ABOUT THE AUTHOR

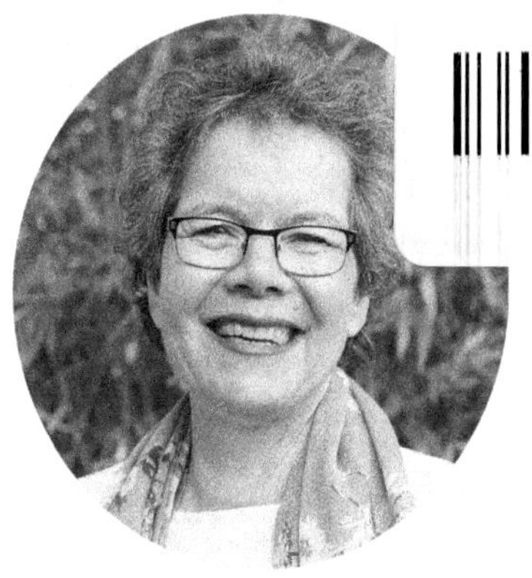

Tessa is a coach for Highly Creative Persons as well as a career and executive coach. She is specialised in aiding her clients find ways to channel their creative genius – whether they have been diagnosed as highly creative or whether wishing to re-connect to this inherently human super power.

Having learned to deal with the gift of being highly creative in a world that does not understand nor appreciate this gift, she is now a sought-after expert in how to channel creativity in all walks of life, whether in our professional life, artistic creation, creative healing or finding meaning. Intrigued by the question of what we humans can accomplish and what triggers our full potential, she travelled the outer and inner worlds, exploring and developing practices that help to tap into our full human potential. These include forms of meditation, autogenic training, shamanism and mindset techniques used by top athletes, as well as artistic flow and other states of consciousness we experience in music.

Before starting to work in the business arena, Tessa was a professional classical musician, performing at a high international level, composing and teaching for more than 30 years. In her second career as a professional artist, during which time her work was exhibited and sold internationally, she learned how images convey information and energy, how they have a profound impact on us, and how we can use them to our advantage in times of crisis and when facing challenges.

As a consequence of how we connect with our essence and with spirit when we are deeply creative, Tessa has also worked as a spiritual counsellor. Creative expression for her is a way of being in the world, one which connects us with the world around us as much as with each other through forms of love.

Feeling spiritually at home in nature, Tessa is a tree hugger and enjoys swimming in lakes as soon as the sun comes out, even during winter.

OUR SECRET POTENTIAL by Tessa Richter

40 years exploring and teaching the benefits of music, meditative states of flow, artistic creation, mindfulness, meditation, and mindset techniques. Coaching professionals to find their voice, meaning and purpose, and to perform at top level. Coaching individuals and groups on how to deal with stressful situations and change, and reframe crises in a positive manner to create health, happiness and purpose, leading to more success in all areas of life.

Being Highly Creative

Our superpower at the dawn of a new era

Tessa I. Richter

Thank you, Margie, for being the initiator to this book. Thank you, Louise, for your unending support with editing. I cannot thank you enough for your generosity. Thank you, mysterious inner pulse of my life, for having taken me to where I am now. I am in awe of how you weave your magic.

Thank you, creative life force, for expressing through me in so many ways. Your twists and turns never cease to amaze me. I cannot wait to see where you take me next. Thank you, my reader, for being curious enough about one of the greatest gifts we possess.

CONTENTS

INTRODUCTION

Wishing that, during my life, I had had someone by my side to help me understand why I am the way I am and tell me that I am loveable exactly as I am, I started out writing this book for those of you with the same gift: high creativity. While I was writing, I realised that what highly creative individuals experience is essentially possible for all of us, and that anyone can really benefit from my findings.

At the dawn of a new era, the gift of being highly creative – one that we all possess inherently - is a blessing. It can help us as we are confronted with unprecedented challenges and the ever-increasing power of AI.

This book is for anyone wishing to (re-) connect with their superpower of high creativity, to understand this gift, to channel its potent energy and create a new world for all of us. It has evolved naturally from my last book "Our Secret Potential" which introduced the idea that we are using only a fraction of our human potential due to misconceptions about us as human beings and because of an outdated view of the world we live in. It also talked about this particular aspect of our unused potential. Since I now realise being highly creative is my most potent "secret potential" I have decided to dedicate an entire book to the subject.

Those of you who have read my last book will recognise some of the ideas and stories. Our fast-paced world wants something new and exciting at every turn; we seem to need a "fix" of new ideas and news at an increasingly faster pace. That is how we are being fed by the media.

Here, however, I am leading you towards new territory, this time on a profound and existential level. And because it is so new and unheard of, it is worth hearing more than once. Also, when a story is repeated, it is under a new angle, not yet explored, as stories are multifaceted ways of transporting wisdom and understanding.

Just as we have learned to view the world we live in through innumerable repetitions of the same ideas, through our educational system, our upbringing and the society we live in, the new paradigm that is emerging at the dawn of a new era, needs many repetitive loops to engrave itself and overlay the old paradigm.

Think of it like listening to music you love and that brings you peace and joy every single time. This is the kind of book you can read over and over again. There are many layers to understanding and integrating what is being presented.

RE-CONNECTING TO OUR INHERENT GENIUS

We are all born highly creative

A study done by Nasa in 2020 found that 98% percent of 5-year-old children fall into the "genius category of imagination". This number dropped to 12% for 15-year-olds and to 2% for adults. What we can take from this is that our current educational system at home, school and university, and the predominant skills we learn during professional training, are making us totally un-creative.

At the brink of a new era of humanity, standing at an abyss that could well end our life on this planet, let me take a moment to reflect on how we've come here, and how we could possibly move forward.

Our educational system is, of course, based on our view of the world we live in, on hundreds of years of rational science that only focuses on what is measurable, material and quantifiable. We have eradicated all that is human out of the equation: nature, spirit, soul, a greater intelligence. Ultimately, we have cut ourselves off from our deepest roots as human beings, in trying to create machines that are controllable and predictable. We are now seeing the consequences of this approach to our world and our human nature: mental stress-related diseases are getting out of control and making health costs explode without solving the problem in any way. We have reduced Nature and the Earth to a commodity, not understanding that nature is who we are, it is part of us and we are a part of her. We put plasters on festering wounds by teaching people to meditate and by recycling material. However, unless we understand that our "operating system" of humans as better machines is outdated, we will not be able to bring about substantial change for the better.

Our creative genius is our innate superpower that can get us beyond this abyss into a new world. A world which we will be proud to be a part of and live in. This is a place where we no longer operate from the need to control and compete, out of fear and a feeling of scarcity. We will understand that, based on a new emerging view of the world, with the new "operating system" of quantum physics, that we are all interconnected with all that exists, and that what we believed to be solid matter does not exist. In this new world there is no real scarcity, there is an abundance of love, trust and cooperation. No-one needs to go hungry because a few of us are hoarding commodities and controlling the financial market based on greed, a product of fear.

Creative intelligence is one of the most essential keys to this new world. When I talk about creativity, I mean so much more than coming up with yet another idea of how to make more profit by inventing a new product or gadget that is not essential or how to exploit nature for the soul purpose of human greed.

I propose to take you to unchartered territory, where magic is possible, because we will have learned to use not just our heads and analytical brains, but our hearts and guts as well. We will have changed our wiring entirely to connect all aspects of who we are, and in so doing will have regained our in-born genius.

This genius and new form of creativity is already present in today's world, but not yet well known. It is expressed in simple solutions to the energy crisis as proposed by farmers in the US, portrayed in the film 'The Need to Grow': restoring all the nutrients and superpower to the earth, growing vegetables, and creating enough energy through this process for the needs of a house, and on a larger scale for a community. No waste material, no mining, no transport. Simply nature.

This is the kind of creativity we need, one that understands how we all interconnect with each other and the planet we live on. If we disregard these factors, creativity can cause havoc. An example of this is the creation of solar collectors which require battery mining. They cause incredible amounts of waste and kill off the most vital wild parts of our earth. Yet they are at the heart of a proposed Swiss government emergency plan in the Swiss alps.

Entering the realm of creativity is opening up to the present. Totally. With no safety net. This may well challenge you beyond anything you know on all levels: your mind, your concepts and your emotions.

Being creative is our journey to wholeness. It is reconnecting with our deepest roots as human beings: nature, spirit and soul - and the heart.

Being a Highly Creative Person

Some of us have somehow managed, in spite of prevailing beliefs and education, to stay connected with that genius part of us. We live a life that is often misunderstood, and therefore judged and belittled. Our values are very far from what most people believe and desire.

Being highly creative is a unique way of being in the world, one you don't ever want to miss once you've tasted it.

Perhaps what made me preserve my precious gift of high creativity was having to adapt to so many different environments, cultures and languages. This may have allowed me to keep making new creative connections in my brain, unlike maybe children who grow up in a constant environment. Add to this the privilege of being born into an intellectual family, where both parents went to university and spoke several languages, and also being given the opportunity to learn music – even two instruments -, horse riding, ice skating, tennis and other extra-curricular activities.

It took me many years to realise that I am highly creative, and even when I was diagnosed as such, I didn't really believe it nor know how to react. I lived most of my life feeling like I'm from a different planet and don't know how things work here on this one. And I've spent most of my life living alone, easily overwhelmed by the demands of everyday life, earning a living and caring for myself on a physical level.

It has taken most of my life to understand there is absolutely nothing wrong with me. Our Western world is simply not geared towards people like me. As the neuropsychologist said who diagnosed me: being highly creative is extremely difficult in today's Western world. The challenges are not understood by others, and it's not easy learning to function in a world based on a totally different perspective of human beings and a different way of functioning.

I finally understand that I am a reservoir of inexhaustible creative energy, and any issues of mental and physical health I may have come from bottling up this energy, not allowing it to flow freely, or not finding an appropriate channel for this universal energy which is as potent as love.

I am writing this in the hope of inspiring all of you to open up to this precious gift we all possess, as well as for those of you who have already uncovered it. It is neither easy nor simple.

Being highly creative is perhaps the greatest challenge of your life, but also the greatest blessing, which brings with it rewards you couldn't dream of – ever. It is not for the fainthearted.

But you probably already know that if you've begun the journey of expressing who you are in today's world. Confronted with its challenging aspects of rejection, being misunderstood, not belonging, whilst battling our inner daemons of worthlessness, doubt and inferiority, there seem to be two choices: conform to the norm and hide this gift away in the depth of oblivion, or express it and be lonely. Either way, I feel cut off. Cut off from myself and the incredible potential I carry inside me. Or cut off from the rest of the world because I am different by my very nature.

Being highly creative is not just a gift I can choose to express or not. It is a way of traveling through life, approaching situations, getting things done, and even of connecting the spiritual with the material. It colours every single aspect of my life, my being. Everything I do and don't do. Every single decision.

So, what is the blessing, you may ask?

Using our creative energy is plugging into the current of the universe, connecting our heart and soul to dimensions of existence that are mystical, deeply moving and fulfilling.

Expressing creativity is a way to enter other worlds, other states of consciousness. Some of these I first experienced as a teenager, through listening to music and practicing it myself. I learned to label these much later as ecstasy and trance. Both states are more commonly known to be reached through religious or spiritual practices, like in shamanism and ancient tribal ceremonies. Or through drugs of both healing and hallucinatory nature. In fact, these states of consciousness, as I was to find out, are an important aspect of being highly creative. And part of our human heritage that we have lost.

I was traveling through Europe at the young age of 16 and, having landed in Amsterdam, was offered some hashish. Here was my chance to explore further what I had already experienced in music. Everybody told me how it made listening to music and dancing, as well as the way we perceive colours, more intense. For me, however, it was a let-down. I felt that what I was able to experience without this drug, in music, was more powerful.

How do you get into a state of ecstasy and trance without drugs? This was to become an exploration of a lifetime: I have found similar states in art, music, spiritual practices and love.

Are you a Highly Creative Person?

So, how would you know that you're highly creative? I was 45 when I found out. Once again in a deep crisis and not knowing what to do with my life, I went to see a neuropsychologist for guidance. I wanted help in evaluating my professional future following a successful international career as a classical musician and a second one as an artist, painter and sculptor.

The test I carried out with the counsellor showed me to be highly creative, with a result that less than 1 in 1000 people the same age achieve. As mentioned above, the counsellor also told me that this was one of the most challenging gifts to have and to come to terms with in today's world. That didn't really help.

Here I had been thinking I wasn't particularly creative, perhaps because my creative efforts were never acknowledged as such nor appreciated. I remember, as a teenager, knitting some pretty far-out clothing and wearing it, but also thinking this was just teenager stuff. I also remember doing a maths exam, at quite a high level, shortly before the Matura, the final school exams in Switzerland before going on to university. I managed to work out one of the examination questions in my head and came up with the correct answer. It was marked wrong, because I hadn't shown my path to solving the problem on paper, I had just put down the end result. This made me feel like a complete failure. I was obviously unable to do things the way they were supposed to be done. It is only now I understand that this was my highly creative brain at work. I may add that it was a very typical example of the way a highly creative brain fires away. It is like a firework going off in my brain. I have no control over it, but at the same time I feel intensely focused with a high degree of clarity. Nowadays, when I coach highly trained and skilled specialists, creatives or executives, it is a similar feeling. They often need practical advice and creative solutions, and my brain feels like it's intensely focused and connecting things in the most amazing way to come up with perfect complex solutions. I just love it!

At the time, when I was growing up, there was generally no awareness about people being highly gifted, highly sensitive, creative etc. The concern was more for those who were under average. Even now, when I tell friends that I'm highly gifted, they tend to think "lucky you"! People don't understand the challenges involved, nor the pain and suffering.

It has taken me most of my life to realise that, in fact, I am extremely gifted – through no merit of my own, I may add, for it was given to me - and therefore function in a very different way from most people I know. Certainly different from my teachers and peers. Different from other professional musicians, even different from other artists. And that this is absolutely fine. I deserve to be appreciated, acknowledged and loved for who I am, just as everyone else does.

Getting back to the question of how to find out whether you are highly creative: one way to know if you're highly creative, is to do a test, although currently there is no standard test for this. There are questionnaires and the kind of test I did with my psychologist. Another way is to look at your life. In this case, there is no one criteria that is conclusive. There need to be several indications for it to be somewhat conclusive. If you're not sure, do consult an expert.

Here are some aspects that could indicate that you are a Highly Creative Person, bearing in mind that answering yes to these questions could also mean that you have another "neurodiverse condition" like autism, ADHD, etc.

- *Are you somebody who has had different careers?*
- *Who needs new challenges as soon as you've mastered one?*
- *Who needs to do things differently from others, your own way?*
- *Do you have trouble doing something in exactly the same way over and over again?*

- *Do you have trouble fitting into long working hours every day?*
- *Have you had several severe crises at recurring intervals in your life?*
- *Once you've built a new life for yourself and everything works fine, it suddenly hits you again for no apparent reason and you no longer feel on track?*
- *Have you experienced other states of consciousness, like on drugs, through music, art, nature or love?*
- *Do you experience depressive phases where nothing makes sense?*
- *Can you see behind the obvious? Recognise patterns where others don't?*
- *Are you intense, sometimes too much so for others? With deep emotions?*
- *And are you either obsessive with daily chores, or can't get yourself to do them?*

One strong indicator that you may be highly creative is the desire to express something unique. There is an inner urge to create, on your own terms. To not follow the way other people do things. This can manifest in many different areas of your life and need not be in artistic ventures. Let me give you an everyday example. I never learned to cook, but when I started to do so, I did follow recipes. And I still do for baking. Over the years, living on my own a lot of the time, I have completely changed my style and way of cooking. I throw together things, do new combinations of foods that I think might be nice. I don't want to spend much time on it, but it has to taste good. My close friends are all good cooks and I have felt somewhat inferior because of my way of doing things. I felt my cooking was not up to their standards. Until recently a friend staying with me commented that she admires the fact that my cooking doesn't take long. People do seem to like the taste of my cooking, but I've always assumed it to be inferior because I don't follow strict rules and because I don't take so long.

Highly creative people easily get bored with learning technical skills and with doing things the way they are usually done. However, if you don't master an art, a skill or technique first, as creative as you may be, you will never feel fully content and as though you've achieved your full potential. The challenge is to find a way of becoming a master in your field without losing yourself and your creativity.

Another criterion to being highly creative is having extreme emotional ups and downs such as those a bipolar person experiences. You don't sleep because you're in a state of high and wanting to create, or you're in a state of deep depression when nothing makes sense, and the creative life force has run dry. I have a highly creative friend who gets so down she gets alarmingly ill with the worst symptoms. And all of a sudden, they just disappear.

Being in a relationship with a bipolar man for 7 years, I learned a lot from the way he handled, or I should really say, couldn't handle his creative energy. It made me realise that this could have been me, had I not found ways to constructively express this powerful energy. At the time I just struggled with this relationship. It was only later, after having done research on bipolar musicians, that I realised there was a connection.

In a phase of creative flow you can be the happiest person, creating in a state of trance, taking you to the heights of ecstasy. In a stagnant phase, on the other hand, you can feel thoroughly depressed, incapable and despondent. People can become suicidal at this stage, not seeing where and when the creative juices will flow again.

I have come to see both aspects as being equally necessary and valid parts of my life. Every creative process has its ups and downs, its stagnating and flowing phases. There are no shortcuts and we will experience both.

For a highly creative person, life is often much more intense, and therefore more challenging than for others. Even to the point of being ominous and threatening. The good news is that there are ways to deal with it without becoming mentally ill.

Besides conventional methods to establish your degree of creative talent, there are also more unorthodox and perhaps controversial means, which helped me recognise who I am. I will share two of them here. One is my blood type. I found that mine, type B, deals best with stress by being creative.

Another way I investigated life and its laws, was numerology. Like astrology, this is an ancient art that goes back thousands of years to a time when our ancestors were more connected to the inherent laws of the universe on an instinctual and spiritual level, whereas today we tend to connect more through the head and through science. Humans, then, felt themselves to be part of the world around them, as one.

In exploring numerology, I found that, if you have a double 1, i.e. an 11 in a prominent place in your numerology chart, chances are that creativity is a key element in your life. If you have more than one 11, then you could well be highly creative - I have 3.

Why am I sharing this very personal information at the risk of being ridiculed? It was my very own investigation into who I am, my personal validation and support, which kept me going when there was no-one to turn to. It was these mirrors along the way that validated my essence. I encourage you to find your own validation and support best suited to who you are and what you love and adapted to your lifestyle. If your creative genius expresses through movement, you may want to find a different mirror in the outside world to confirm what you feel on the inside, from someone who loves cooking, speaking in public or setting up their own business. In any case, it is about finding that necessary support on your journey to your essence.

For those of you interested in finding out more, I have created an assessment to evaluate whether or not you are highly creative. Alongside an extensive questionnaire, we will look at relevant aspects of your life.

UNDERSTANDING THIS SUPERPOWER

Intelligence and driving force

The math incident I described above not only illustrates how, as a Highly Creative Person, you are different and can feel inadequate, but it also illustrates an important aspect of creativity that most people are not aware of.

When asked what being highly creative means, you would probably answer: someone who is artistic, someone who is a prolific creator of art or craft. But that is only one of many different ways high creativity can be expressed. Being artistic per se is not an act of creativity, unless you create something entirely new that did not exist before. Otherwise, it is an act of artistic expression, a skill like talking or doing sports, one that can be learned and practised.

Being highly creative is actually a form of intelligence. Intelligence being defined here by connections in our brain. The more we connect and make new connections in our brains, the more creative intelligence we possess.

If creativity is a form of wiring in the brain, this means it is also a way to perceive the world around us. Being highly creative enables us to change perspective easily. We can look at things in many different ways, not just in the way everybody else is used to.

By looking at our world in another way, reality actually changes, it becomes different. While this may seem an awesome ability, it can actually be quite disconcerting. Things for a highly creative person are not fixed as they are for most people. And talking to someone for whom reality is one reality only, can be a profoundly disturbing experience for someone with this ability. You are literally living in different worlds.

Besides being a form of intelligence and a way of perceiving the world we live in, creativity is also a form of energy, a force of nature. As such it is part of the human condition, of who we are intrinsically: each and every one of us creates new cells in our bodies every single day of our lives. On a less physical level, creativity is an energy we can connect with, like love. In itself it is not positive or negative. It is pure energy and up to us to channel it. It has the ability to transport us to our highest heights and lowest depths.

If we don't learn to channel our superpower, it can go stale and create havoc. We can create „healthy" cells in our bodies or „sick" ones. And we can create something that is perceived as valuable and nurturing or worthless and destructive.

Creative potential, like any other potential, needs to be expressed in some way. If not, we will not feel well, both mentally and physically, and we may even get sick.

Creativity at work...

Creativity may well be one of the most sought-after skills and talents in the decades to come, as AI (Artificial Intelligence) takes over many, if not most, of our day-to-day manual tasks and, increasingly, even the more complex ones. Who would once have thought it possible for a car to drive itself?

For us highly creatives this is good news. Our place in this technological universe, in what is termed the fourth industrial revolution, could be crucial for humanity.

Educational thinkers believe that the arts and creativity could become more important for young people than maths in the future. According to them, we will need more skills gained through creativity than through test-based learning, maths and science.

Recently, a friend told me about an experiment whereby three composers produced music in the style of Bach: the composer himself, a modern composer who imitated him, and AI. Professionals then listened to assess which music was by whom. The result was that many thought AI was Bach, Bach was the modern composer and the modern composer AI. In other words, it was not clear who had authored what.

In this day and age when we are still in awe of the capacities of AI, this can seem amazing to many. However, there is a hitch. While AI can produce music that is complex enough to make it indistinguishable from the original, it would never ever come up with the original music. Only Bach himself, a real person, living at a specific time in history, in a specific place, can be the inspired source of his music, in a style that is unique and highly complex, as well as uplifting and deeply satisfying for the mind and the heart. AI cannot do this.

AI can imitate and perhaps be more perfect than the original, it can copy in endless variations. It is never inspired, it doesn't have access, as we do, to intuition, to the erratic loopholes of creativity and to inspiration.

And by the way, AI will never know what love is, even if it is excellent at imitating loving behaviour. I find this deeply comforting. Humans will not be made "redundant" by "better humans." And creativity is one of those key fundamentally human skills.

As humans, we are able to connect and access other states of consciousness, experienced in a state of flow while being creative. It is what some artists and musicians call connecting to the divine or spirit, what I like to call the mysterious inner pulse. In scientific terms, it is connecting to the Field, a concept I will share more about later.

Before we get practical, allow me to introduce you to some insights and more abstract findings, which I believe will make a huge difference when you set out on your own creative journey. Many people fail in their creative endeavours because they don't know enough about the nature of creative processes. They give up just before achieving what they set out to do.

By looking at art and observing nature, we can learn much about the process of creativity at work, at how it evolves. Both nature and art yield valuable insights and will allow us to identify useful tools and approaches.

… in nature

How does nature create new life? New branches on a tree?

All of us, including plants and animals, can only grow according to our inherent nature. There is some kind of seed that contains the genetic material, the blueprint of what is possible and what is not. Often it is fertilised or needs to be planted in the right environment. It grows, as all things in nature do, in cooperation with its environment, getting food and nourishment from the elements around it. Latest scientific research shows that even trees in a forest cooperate! They communicate underground with their roots and, it seems, they actually watch out for each other and other plants like mushrooms around them.

In a world of feasibility, driven by machines and computers, where everything seems to be possible everywhere and at all times, one thing we can learn from observing how nature creates, something modern humans have forgotten about, are the elements of place, environment and time.

Every being, every plant, stone, element of nature has its own rhythm and cycle. And so do we. So do our creations. There is, indeed, a time for everything. Timing is crucial and will sometimes be the decisive factor in birthing a creation or not.

A seed takes its time, it does not grow faster if I watch it grow, dig it up to see if it's really progressing, or if I give it more of what it needs. It has its own inherent timing and rhythm. It also has its inherent needs in terms of environment and nourishment. Things in nature will not grow independently of their inherent cycle of growth. Yet, humans are expected to do so. And there are various stages each living being, whether mineral, plant or animal, goes through. No stage can be left out. This is important to remember when we're dealing with our own creativity.

I've found that any project or work of art, in other words things we want to create, to be like plants or babies. There is a kind of conception, the actual birth, a phase of growing up and finally leaving home. It is important to understand what stage of this process our creation is at. This will determine what our project needs: more nurturing, a form of communication, sending it out into the world for others to see or interact with...?

The first phase in nature is planting a seed in the right environment. In terms of plants this would be soil, sun, water. In human terms this could be creating space and time for our endeavour, learning, developing and practicing a new skill, preparing the canvas so to speak. Then there is a time of gestation. Perhaps we need to do more research, develop another skill, or wait for someone to give us information or join our project. Or we're simply not sure how to proceed.

Many people give up at this stage of their undertaking, because they think the seed is dead. It is actually alive and growing, but not necessarily visibly so. The creative current has gone underground, needing to be nurtured while incubating. Like with any natural being, no amount of will power will make it grow faster than it is "programmed" to do by its inherent nature.

Translated to my life and projects, there are many aspects determining the right time: the overall cycle of my life, my capacity and resources, but perhaps also inherent characteristics and conditions of the project itself. Sometimes, the timing is off with people, the world around us: we can be ahead of our time with our ideas.

When starting out, the "baby", the new life of a project, idea or work, needs to be nourished without squashing it or exposing it to harsh influences. In the infant stages where you can already see first little "sprouts", it is still vital to protect it. Don't go telling everyone you're now an artist or you now have your own business, or whatever it is you're creating. People always want to see results and judge you if you have nothing to show. The same is true when you're in a process of healing, having found your own path, whether conventional, alternative or spiritual.

Others don't always get what you're about. They will want to advise and interfere, with the best of intentions. This energy in turn falls back on you and can be very discouraging. Treasure your new endeavour, the new you, and only give it away to whom you trust with your life! Treat it like you would your precious own offspring at its early stage of being a baby.

Later on, if you don't like the result, or are not quite happy how it's developing, treat your creation like a baby or child that you would never "give back" or exchange for another one. Rather you love it for who and what it is, and you do what you can to help it become its very best. Ask yourself: what can I do to help it grow in the best possible manner? What exactly could be done to nurture it so it can thrive?

Don't destroy the whole thing just because it's not what you expected it to be. Perhaps at a later time, you may like what you created, because you can look at it from a different angle. It may have taught you something about yourself from a new perspective, or an unusual aspect is suddenly in vogue and you're getting great feedback.

Think of what we create in terms of it being like children growing up, challenging us beyond anything we've been able to conceive of so far, broadening our horizon and helping us gain a new perspective on life.

… and in art

Art is a great playground to experience creativity at work. It is not, really not, any more valid than any other creative processes. But it does enable us to look at many aspects of the human creative process over a period of time.

Just like in nature, in art there is also a seed, a suitable environment and appropriate timing. What is perhaps the greatest difference, and one that is a key to human creativity, is self-awareness. With it come inspiration and choice. For many artists there is some greater force at work. They see themselves as channels, inspired by some greater force, whether they call it God, inspiration, or universal intelligence. They are aware of "receiving" their works. In many respects the process is one of conceiving and giving birth, like women do with children.

In modern times, as we have become removed and detached from nature, using it as a commercial resource, we have also come to believe we can be God-like: so self-centred that we believe we can create exactly what we want, without taking into consideration the greater good, our environment, our very own nature or other aspects of creation.

Through creating artistically and looking at my own life in terms of an inspired work of art, I have come to believe in the concept of co-creating, the idea that we are not sole creators of our life, but that we co-create our lives with an intelligent greater force.

I was inspired to this approach by my sculpting process, where I co-operated with the stones I was working on. Here, I found that, rather than imposing my own idea of what the sculpture should look like, I could work together with the stone, i.e. its colour, texture and other attributes. I allowed these aspects to influence the direction of my chiselling and shaping. Not only was this a very fulfilling and rewarding way of working, the result was that of organic "beings". Personally, I've always found it odd to see heads of people or busts, just cut off randomly.

Whether you are a confirmed Highly Creative Person or setting out to explore your innate creative genius that has been lost, artistic creation is a great practicing and playing ground. We can later apply its principles and processes to creating other aspects of our lives, and even good health. The creative energy is not limited to our artistic expression, but it can be safely channelled here, where it cannot do any harm. Artistic creativity can give us a sense of trying something new and finding new ways of expressing ourselves. We can go into new territory in a safe and supportive environment. We experience ourselves in the creative process, what it's like to be in flow, perhaps even trance and ecstasy. The medium you express in is of no importance, whatever you feel drawn to most: writing, drawing, sound or movement. Expressing yourself this way breaks down limitations, sets energy free and can give you a sense of achievement, regardless of the outcome, if you approach it that way.

One of the most important lessons and experiences gained by the creation of art, is connecting to our very own essence, the seed that we came into this world with. It is about uncensored and non-judgemental pure expression of the self and the divine.

Modern physics and the act of creating

More and more people, especially physicists, biologists, but also business professionals and those engaged in the cultural sector, are becoming interested in the findings of modern physics as a base for a different perspective on everyday life and the world we live in.

We have grown up believing in a three-dimensional and linear world, based on Newton's laws. Linear denotes a relationship of cause and effect, one incident causing another.

Modern physics challenges this view and literally moves us towards an entirely new world. The good news is that this will enable us to deal with many of the challenges our world faces today in a more appropriate and positive manner.

For Highly Creative People, this view is more in line with the way we actually perceive the world around us. We do not experience the world as solely linear and three-dimensional.

The most fascinating theories of modern physics are the Quantum Theory, the Field Theory and the Morphogenetic Fields of Rupert Sheldrake. I also found much interesting food for thought in the Science of Chaos, confirming some of the insights I had when I let myself be inspired by nature. Though not strictly scientific, I would also like to include the psychologist C.G. Jung with his concept of synchronicity, a phenomenon which I have observed time and again in my own life and which is explicable through modern physics.

Let us begin with Quantum Physics. In its findings, it is said that a particle is both a wave and a particle at the same time. If it is observed, the location is fixed and it becomes a particle. Otherwise, it exists in a kind of ambivalent, original state as a wave.

Translated into our everyday lives, this means that reality is directly linked with an observer, and that what I observe becomes reality. We co-create reality at the very core of matter. Where my focus goes is where my reality unfolds.

Subatomic particles are, moreover, capable of communicating and cooperating with each other. They are so closely linked with each other that they communicate across great distances, without loss of time. Spatial and temporal separation do not exist on this level: the information is in different places at the exact same time. This is called the phenomenon of simultaneousness. In my opinion this is the basis for what Jung calls synchronicity.

Jungs' "synchronicity", as opposed to causality, is the application of the scientific insights of Quantum Theory to the human psyche. It was always assumed that events in our lives were connected through a causal chain, one event causing another. As in physics, so in psychology.

Jung observed that events can be connected synchronistically, without one of them having caused the other. This phenomenon is often perceived as a coincidence in our everyday life: the phone rings just as we are thinking of someone, or we are concerned with a question and somebody, even without knowing it, gives us a hint or an answer. This also explains why inventions are made in different places, all over the world, at the exact same time.

Regarding life as a simple chain of cause and effect, of immovable facts and fixed objects has become obsolete. Everything is vibration and all is interconnected. Reality no longer exists detached from myself and my perception. So, if I change how I look at the world, this will have a direct impact on my surroundings and eventually on my life and the world I live in. It will literally change my world.

Sheldrake, for his part, speaks of Morphogenetic Fields in which each thought, every feeling and every event is stored. The more people do or think the same, the bigger the corresponding field. He reckoned that proteins and genes can no better explain the physical shape of living beings, than building material on a building site can explain the form of a house. Everything, from molecules and organisms through to societies and galaxies, is determined, in his view, by morphic fields which are connected by resonance with similar systems and fields of all cultures and across all times.

This implies, amongst other things, that the field of a thought becomes bigger the more people think that thought. I find this very comforting, for it means that I do not have to effectuate all innovations myself. It is enough for me to think a certain thought and thereby contribute to spreading it, until the field is so large that it is easy for many people to have this same thought, by tapping into its morphogenetic field. It also explains how certain skills evolve and spread and are more readily accessible to everyone. The bigger the field of a certain skill, the more people are capable of it and the easier it is for anyone to tap into it.

The Field theory takes this idea a step further, combining many different findings of science. It assumes that there is one Field that connects all that exists. All existing information is contained in this Field and everything determines and influences everything else. Through this Field we have access to any information that exists in the present, the past and the future. This, of course, enhances the idea of each of us being co-responsible, a fact we are more and more becoming aware of through ecology and the world-wide-web.

The idea of the Field could actually be where modern physics meets ancient spiritual traditions, and it might be what mystics such as Krishnamurti experience directly in their entrancement, when they say: „You are the world".

For me, the most revolutionary idea of the Field is that memory is not something inside of us, but that the brain is an instrument with which we can retrieve any information we need from the Field. So instead of "thinking" we would be "receiving". According to this theory, we would be in a kind of constant interaction with the Field, and this would also explain creativity, intuition and inspiration. And this is where it becomes very relevant for us when dealing with the creative force. Communicating with the Field, with universal dimensions, can help us find solutions, ideas and orientation, and help us make the right decisions. It enables us to be in a kind of life flow, intuitively being in the right place at the right time.

For a Highly Creative Person it is good to know there is some guidance, a compass out there, with which we can connect, as we can easily get lost in the chaos of our creative impulses.

Simply connecting to the Field will mean connecting to all the possibilities out there. When we connect to the Field through the lens of our purpose, we make a selection that helps us prioritise. We gain meaning and focus, can achieve undreamed of feats, and create what is meant for us.

We co-create the world we live in

Applying what I learned from modern physics to my life and my art has greatly helped me to not go crazy or to completely get lost. I now understand that life is like a partner. This partner has its own rhythm, its own inherent intelligence, and I need to trust it. What I learned, is that cooperation works best. I call this: co-creating with life as it is.

It may seem frustrating at first, but actually, it is liberating not to be the sole responsible creator. It enables me to let go, I can hand over to a higher form of intelligence and energy than my conscious self, a force that has many more options and is far more creative than I will ever be.

This greater intelligence, whatever you'd like to call it, manifests itself through us directly. If we can learn to get out of its way, it will help us manifest what we wish to create by enhancing and magnifying our very essence. It will help us find the most suited way forward, both in our creations and in our lives. It actually needs us to manifest ourselves on this Earth, as much as we need it. It cannot create without us, and we create on a whole new level together.

This may well be a new concept for many of you and you may be wondering how on earth to know when it's "just me" and when it's universal intelligence. This is indeed a very valid question!

There is an inner feeling, an inner knowing when something is right, when it feels right, not just from my selfish little self, but from a higher perspective. I believe we have all felt this at some point in our lives. My body can be a good indicator: this week I had a challenging decision to make regarding taking on more work. My head was telling me you need to take everything you can get, but it really stressed me. I listened to my body and my soul and set a boundary. I would only take on as much as I sensed was right for me. After that I felt calm inside, strong and centred. We will see later how what I did was crate coherence between my three brains.

Co-creating with the creative life force enables ways of getting us to where we want to go that we could never imagine in our wildest dreams. Understanding that we co-create our projects, our world and everything else, also takes away a lot of unnecessary pressure.

Always trust the process and the creative life force, even if you don't understand it, don't agree or would like things to be different!

Loopholes of creativity: where universal intelligence enters into the game

If we look at life as our co-creating partner, you may wonder how it enters the process in practical terms. An answer to this question can be found in the theory of chaos. Did you know that a healthy heart has a slightly irregular beat? I saw this depicted in a book on the Science of Chaos. The representation of a perfectly regular heartbeat was that of a patient who died a few days later, and the picture with some deviations was that of a healthy heart. I was convinced that it should have been the other way around.

In other words, nothing in nature is ever as precise as a machine or a computer. It is the small gaps of irregularity that account for our lives, for us being alive and not dead.

The science of chaos offers clues as to how we can co-create our lives in these small gaps and loopholes. Most of us, including myself, have an idea of what we'd like to create when we start out, and get upset if we can't express things the way we want to, or don't achieve the desired result in our projected time frame. We believe that a great artist knows what they are doing, can reproduce certain results infinitely, and that they will produce exactly what they set out to do.

However, if someone reproduces the exact same image/sound or other creation, this is an acquired skill that takes thousands of hours of practice. It is not a creative act in itself.

Creative expression requires training and a high level of expertise. And it happens spontaneously and at a specific moment in time. In the West we have come to value reproducibility and feasibility. This is what a machine does. The prevailing opinion is that if we fail, it is our own fault, our lack of dedication or lack of technical dexterity. This is how we have learned to accomplish what we desire.

For a Highly Creative Person, and therefore potentially for any human being, this is pure poison. What if there is another, more harmonious way to achieve with ease and in keeping with who we are? While technique and full engagement are essential, they are but one aspect of creating. I've found that real satisfaction and fulfilment come from giving it all I have in terms of energy, technical skills etc, and then allowing the unintentional to enter into it, to do its part.

This means that one extremely important aspect of being a channel for creation, is the ability to step out of the way, to allow the unintentional to enter the creative process.

Whilst this cannot actually be planned, it is important to acknowledge it as an integral part of any creative process. Many great artists and composers call this God, I would call it Spirit, greater intelligence, universal energy, or simply life.

Allowing the unintentional to co-create in our projects, in life as in art, makes for surprises and results we could never have dreamed of in our wildest dreams.

To illustrate how this greater creative life force enters into our creative processes, let me share an experience I had myself, visible in the picture below. I was filming my statue "Sarasvati, the goddess of rivers, art, music and wisdom", when suddenly I saw the goddess of the river appear in the stone next to her - here she is on the right. It was the most amazing awe-inspiring moment!

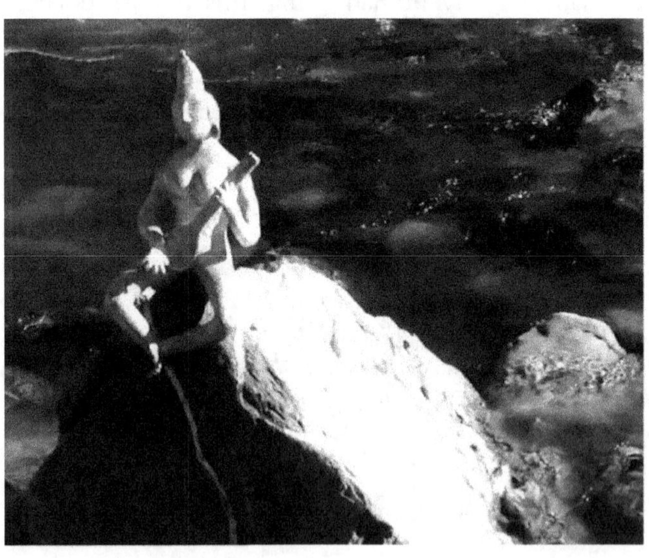

This phenomenon happens not only in artistic creative processes, but also in all areas of life, including healing physically or mentally. Here, this unintentional is termed spontaneous healing. When doctors and scientists can't find a rational explanation why someone is healed from an incurable disease or without any medical intervention, they have, in the past, mostly chosen to ignore it. But this aspect of healing is now beginning to receive some attention. It is in fact the phenomenon of the unintentional, of Spirit entering into what we are creating. It is also the inherent intelligence our bodies and soul possess that we don't really understand or appreciate yet.

Please allow all this information to sink in deeply. Not only will it change how you view the world, it will allow you to begin living in a different world. In this world, things function in a different manner and the unimaginable becomes possible. As Highly Creative People we need this new perspective and perception in order to fully develop our creative potential. Our genius cannot thrive in the old paradigm.

I am glad that life will always offer us loopholes of creativity, translating into unplanned experiences which cause a range of feelings, from devastating to uplifting. I believe that unforeseeable experiences carry a great treasure which a large part of our culture draws from in art and music, but which, sadly, most of our society tries to eliminate. It is perceived at best as esoteric, spiritual, artsy, but nothing to depend on, and to be avoided at all cost. Because it means acknowledging a greater force than ourselves. And our scientific mind has come to believe in humans and AI as "the crowning glory of creation":

The loopholes of creativity represent the place where free will, inspiration, evolution and creativity are located. As such they may be that aspect of being human that can take us to another level of intelligence and help solve the many challenges we are facing today.

Just imagine the universe unfolding and evolving exactly as man conceived it. What a disaster that would be! We all know and we've all experienced the fact that life does not stick to our plans. Yet, we are still brought up to believe that we can control what happens in our lives and that, if we are currently facing ill fate, it is because we did something wrong. But what if we simply don't have that power? What if there is an element of chaos, of unpredictability, as we have seen in the creative process? An element that seems chaotic, yet wise and super-intelligent at the same time?

Let us then assume that life is on our side. That these loopholes of creativity are places where universal intelligence enters into the game. And that this greater force actually wants us to succeed, to be happy and healthy, to create what really matters in our lives, for ourselves and those around us.

I have come to realise that believing this will give my life so much more meaning, and myself so much more power in dealing with hardship or with any kind of problem. Everything takes on another meaning, seems more worthwhile. I truly believe that life is our partner and wants only the very best for us. Because life is so much greater than me, because universal intelligence can come up with so many more unbelievable paths I would have never dreamt of. Why not trust it? And unwrap the gifts it is putting in front of me – in whatever shape or form?

CHANNELING OUR SUPERPOWER

Dealing with a mixed blessing

Most people would probably think of being highly creative simply as having tons of creative energy. I actually believe that there is not just a quantitative difference between being creative and being highly creative. There is a quantum leap from one to the other, a shift into another, multidimensional reality, a bit like shifting gears, a new dimension altogether, where creativity plays out in different networks, areas of our brains and our other brains, heart and gut, all at once. That is why it is so challenging and rewarding at the same time.

When I was a teenager, I was wondering one day what would happen if I closed my eyes while driving on my little moped, on a stretch of road that was completely straight. No sooner had I thought this, than I put it into practice - and woke up in hospital. I don't actually remember getting there. I have often wondered about this. Until I started writing about being highly creative in an article preceding this book, I had no clue why I would do such a thing. I hadn't considered creativity to be a form of intelligence, therefore connected to my head. I don't know where I would have located it, but definitely not in the head.

Looking back at that time, I remember feeling under pressure, depressed, lost. From my present-day perspective, I realise that some of the pressure was this energy wanting to be expressed. At the time, I didn't know how to. In an attempt to deal with it, I tried to switch my head off. I thought there was something wrong with me, and I wanted it to stop. We had only just moved to Switzerland at the time, and my parents were going through issues that ultimately led to their divorce. This meant they were busy with their own problems. There was no-one to turn to.

If we look at creativity as being a form of energy and being highly creative as having lots of this energy, we can understand how this can be a blessing and a curse at the same time. It will depend on how we learn to utilise and channel this energy, which one it turns out to be. And there will be periods of both in a Highly Creative Person's life.

To channel this energy on a practical level, an important question will be: how can we create a conducive environment for ourselves? What are the conditions we need to manage this gift, and ideally, to thrive in?

There are, in my opinion, two equally important factors. One is space. Space meaning both time to yourself and a physical space to create. You need it when the urge to create grabs you. And, once you're in the flow of creativity, you need the space to follow the path on which this creative energy wants to take you. In this space, you're in your own inner world.

Other people may not understand this vital aspect of who you are, this absolute necessity for time and space. Nor can they fully understand the richness of the inner world of a Highly Creative Person, and how fulfilling and rewarding it is to be there. It will be your job to ensure you have the right conditions for yourself and that they are not negotiable.

Being highly creative means constantly looking at things in new ways, it is exhausting. It is also destabilizing. One can easily get lost.

I have found structure, besides space, to be the second key element in dealing with this gift. Create structures for your days, for your creative processes, as well as for dealing with difficult situations.

And don't question them when you're in the midst of a situation, feeling like you don't know what to do. That is when your creative brain will want to kick in most: to solve the problem. Stay within the structure and allow things to sort themselves in your head and heart without too much pressure. This will leave some of your creative energy for other necessary things, like daily life, as well as for your actual creative endeavours, and it will help keep you grounded, as well as connected to yourself.

Sticking to a form of structure, to a routine to some extent, enables our brain to restructure, regroup itself in times of overload. Many inventors and scientists find the solution to their constant re-search in a moment when they are busy with mundane activities, like taking a shower, driving a car, going for a walk. My own strategies include writing, reading, going for walks, physical exercise, in the summer going to the lake, into the water. And an important thing I've learned is: just do it, even if you don't feel like it.

Besides space and structure, what else can help us create? For me, things need to be tidy and organised in my home and my workplace. When I am in my flat or studio, I need everything to be in its place. Why? Because if it isn't, that triggers ideas of what I could/should be doing. It distracts me and takes up my energy. The same is true for day-to-day chores. They need to be structured in such a way they don't interfere too much with my inner processes.

Any kind of problem or issues in my relationships, with money or other practical questions, will automatically take up my creative energy because, as mentioned above, being highly creative, my brain(s) automatically do what they're best at: create new connections. All the wirings fire away at once to find solutions to practical issues. And there won't be any energy left for those projects and activities that are vital to me. I have come to accept that this is part of life, and that doing chores is also part of my life. And that sometimes I can use my creativity to deal in a new manner with these things.

Besides all this, we do need others.

Here's another paradox: because I require lots of space and time to be on my own, creating, and because I can feel lonely as a result of this, I really need others, in a very existential way. I need friends to ground me, appreciate what I do, support me and cheer me on.

These relationships usually take many years to build. Unfortunately, there is no guarantee they will last and support me when most needed. I have lost many best friends after years of building the relationship. In times of stress, trauma and grief, it would seem, they have felt threatened through the extreme demand on them emotionally. It is too intense, too demanding, too close. The pain that comes from not being understood and abandoned, is another aspect highly creatives have to come to terms with.

And here is another aspect of being highly creative that most people would probably not associate with this gift. Highly Creative People's emotions run very very deep. We have a huge capacity for emotional depth that eludes others. It can easily be misunderstood as unnecessary drama or something others don't want to be a part of. It would seem that being highly creative brings with it not only many dimensions in terms of ideas and energy, but also a whole new dimension of emotions.

Luckily over the course of our lives, there are always new people entering our world, ready and able to love who we are as we evolve. And the more we understand who we are and love ourselves for it, the more we will attract others who are in keeping with us, who love us for who we are. It can also be helpful to find communities of like-minded fellow-creatives. Today's world offers this much more than when I was growing up.

Last but definitely not least: creativity is energy. When you feel under pressure, unable to release, go for a walk, do physical exercise. This will get your ideas and creative processes flowing again. But don't overdo it, or you won't have any energy left to create.

Composition and improvisation – principles of creation

In classical music I had expressed within the given structure of music composed by others. When I began to paint, there were so many possibilities: where do I even start? I gradually developed a style whereby I created my own structure: lines and shapes, derived from a basic form, which would pop into my head before starting the painting. This gave me a point of reference for each painting to come back to and expand from and was actually a lot like composing variations on a theme in music.

I have since evolved in my style and technique, but the basic principle remains: there is always an element of composition upon which I then improvise.

When, many years later, I started composing, I again needed some form of structure. I went to sessions of free improvisation after which I felt lost and unfulfilled, with a headache. Then, similarly to the way I had started painting, I found my way of creating music: an element of composition first, like a series of harmonies, a rhythmic sequence or a melody, and then improvising on this element or elements, recording while I was playing, so as not to lose the spontaneous element. It was finally possible to do so without having to be a technical crack. Sometimes I would write down the compositional elements, the skeleton. Other times, I just had them in my head.

I will not elaborate on all of the techniques I developed, but I kept this basic principle for my varied artistic creations, including writing books. I am sharing this so you can see how the principles of space and structure are applied to a creative process and can thus observe the creative brain at work.

I must add that this is a successful way of functioning only after you've learned your craft and the necessary technical skills. Rather like learning a language with its grammar, phonetics etc., internalising it completely, and then using it to create poetry, lyrics or other creative texts.

Later, I discovered an interesting effect my paintings have on people: a friend, looking at the first painting done in my latest technique, said it looked like when she used to be on drugs as a young woman. Another person who bought a painting said that it enabled her to see between realities, like lifting a veil that separates one dimension from the other. She was able to delve into several dimensions at the same time.

I realised then that I had come full circle. I was now about 50 years old, and had finally managed to translate my experience in music as a teenager, with trance and ecstasy, into visual art. I had accomplished what I set out to do after taking cannabis in Amsterdam. I had found a way to induce this state in others - without drugs.

Being highly creative allows us to move between dimensions, to catch glimpses of what is called Heaven in religion, "ecstasy" with drugs and "other states of consciousness" for shamans and Buddhists. With its help we can create an entirely new world, it will catapult us into a new era where many things are possible that hitherto we have denigrated, laughed upon or pushed away because these phenomena are not controllable by our rational mind and we're afraid of them.

Mysterious inner pulse

Just as music with its beautiful melodies, catchy rhythms and harmonies is held together by its inner pulse, so are we. It is what gives us our unique drive and purpose. This inner pulse is connected to the greater pulse of life, the world around us, to life itself. When these pulses vibrate synchronistically, we experience true magic. Suddenly things materialize, there's serendipity.

If I can tune into my own inner pulse and connect it with the pulse of my life when creating, I will feel supported and in sync.

Modern science tells us that vibration, or pulsation, is the basis for our entire universe. Light, warmth, sound and waves are vibrations. This we know. But there's more.

Everything is alive in our universe and has a pulse. Since, according to Quantum Physics, matter is made up of wave-particles, every thing, being and phenomenon has a pulse, a vibration of its own: all beings, all organic material, organs, cells and even matter which we think of as being "dead". This includes colours, feelings and thoughts.

I call this phenomenon the "mysterious inner pulse", which is at the very core of our being and of everything there is in the universe we live in. The term "mysterious" conveys some of the awe, respect and magic I feel towards life.

These inner pulses are perceived as the spirit of things, situations, places or groups of people, and can also be easily understood with the theory of Sheldrake's morphogenetic fields. We can connect to these fields and gain information about a situation, place etc, and we can communicate with these "spirit-fields-pulses" and interact with them. I would caution you to only do this with an attitude of co-operation and love. Anything else, like wanting to control situations for your own personal benefit and power, will inevitably backfire. So, when you do this, bear in mind the good of everyone involved.

One of the things I came to understand over the course of a creative life, is that every creative process and all creative projects have their own inherent intelligence. By connecting to the inner pulse of a work of art or a business venture, we can gain added information and we can tune into how best to express it.

We have seen above that one aspect of the inner pulse is that everything has its own timing. If you look at your project as you would at a living being, a plant or a tree, you will understand that no amount of willing it to grow or accelerate will change its inherent timing of when it's ready to flourish. This is an aspect we will look at in further detail below. For now, let's understand that creativity doesn't necessarily stick to our wishes and ideas, it comes uninvited. Many times in my life, I have felt like finally things are working out and I can relax, only for life to kick me and force me to move on through an inner impulse to create something new or through some outer from of crisis. This is the inner pulse of my life, of my creativity knocking on the door of my life, wanting me to express something new.

Whereas others spend many years in the same job, I seem to end up building a successful career, only to lose it when I think I've got it. Could this be something innate to Highly Creative People? It's as if we have this in-built creator mechanism that can't settle for repetition and routine. We are built to create. Over and over again.

Being creative is a spiritual experience

In former times, when in need of spiritual advice or emotional support, people went to church or to a temple and prayed. The priestess spoke a wise oracle, or a shaman held a ritual. People believed in destiny, God, or spirits of nature, and if they abided by "their" rules, no harm would come to them, they would be healthy and have all they needed for survival. In those days, people needed someone to translate what these spirits or Goddesses wanted to tell them, wanted them to do or not do. There was a kind of messenger-translator who was more powerful, in that respect, than any other person, because they alone "knew". They were called shamans, priests or oracles.

Today official religions in the West are losing their members. Many people prefer to consult a psychologist when they need help, others find their way to a psychic or a life coach. The yearning for the spiritual remains, and I believe there is a general trend towards spirituality without dogma or an intermediary.

People are searching for a direct personal line to the Divine, the Great Spirit, or whatever you will call this universal aspect. We want to experience this connection first-hand and do not need others claiming to know what is right for us. What we do need, sometimes, are instructions from someone experienced, who knows the way, having been there. I would liken it to a good music teacher who conveys knowledge and techniques, showing me how to play my instrument, but who will not play in my place and will not experience the same feelings in playing as I do, nor will they express who I am. To remain with the image of music making, each person has a gift for a certain instrument, a liking for a certain type of music, and sometimes more than one. The same is true for our spiritual gifts and paths. There is not one way to Spirit, but as many as there are human beings.

Today, we understand that we can connect directly to the universe, Spirit or the mysterious inner pulse. We don't need "connectors" or intermediaries to do it for us. One of the ways to connect to this greater energy is through channelling and expressing our highly creative energy.

This path cannot be explained in terms of a dogma or rules, as it is different for each one of us. We have to start walking on this path to experience it. And like with any walk in nature we don't know in advance what we will encounter on the way. That is part of the magic.

Why is it important to know all this for a Highly Creative Person, or for any other person wishing to connect to this superpower? And what does this mean for us in practical terms?

When we create, whether artistically or in life, we connect with something greater. Many artists call this God. We can also call it the Field, universal intelligence or Spirit. Creating and becoming a channel for creative energy is a highly spiritual act and each one of us will find our own way of doing so. Creating takes us into another dimension of being.

When I, as a Highly Creative Person, talk about the spiritual aspect of creating, the experience of feeling connected and inspired, another highly creative person will often know what I'm talking about. Others may not understand but might have had a comparable experience at church or in nature when they connected to Spirit in another way than through creating.

In order to connect in our own personal way to this larger, greater mystical pulse, we need to know who we are as a channel, as a kind of translator for this greater pulse. What is my language? What is my medium?

A good way to begin is by exploring the mysterious inner pulse of your own life through questions such as:

- *What do I love doing, where do I like to be?*
- *What makes my heart sing?*
- *Who inspires me?*
- *And with what?*

If you're not sure, open yourself to receiving answers both from the inside and from the outside. Our inner pulse speaks to us in the form of impulses, insights and intuition, dreams and daydreams, while we can also receive clues through synchronistic events in the outside world.

What prompted my own journey of spiritual discovery were the experiences I had as a teenager in music, as mentioned earlier. Later on my journey, I experienced how my creative energy was plugging into the current of the universe, connecting me through my heart and soul to dimensions of existence that are mystical and magical.

How do you get into a state of ecstasy and trance without drugs? I knew there was music, I didn't know about all the rest, like shamanism etc. This was to become an exploration of a lifetime, in conjunction with my artistic endeavours. My most recent way of getting "high" has been exploring self-love, as well as a kind of universal, all-encompassing love I have with others.

Expressing our highly creative energy, as well as loving ourselves could actually be the solution to getting off drugs, to becoming independent of any form of addiction. Both activate the same regions in our brain. If we can activate that centre of love for ourselves, we neither need drugs nor someone else to love us.

Many artists, whether painters, musicians or poets, have used drugs or alcohol to get into another state of consciousness to be able to create from another dimension. Shamans use plants and herbal medicine.

What if all of us, as born geniuses gifted with innate high creativity, could access this state without external help? What if that is part of our human potential and heritage? And what if we are finally able to access this superpower because we need it to survive?

USING OUR THREE BRAINS...

If we wish to channel our powerful and intense creative energy so that it gives us joy, fulfilment and a high degree of wellbeing, it will be helpful to understand both where the energy and the inspiration might come from, as well as the "channelling organs" we can use. These include our head brain with its different parts, as well as two more brains which are becoming more and more well known: the heart and the gut. Each of these brains is an access to a certain part of our potential and, as such, a specific means to expressing who we are in our multi-fold dimensions. If we don't use all of these organs it can feel like trying to make a wide river pass through a small, narrow tube.

The brain in our heads is complex and an expression of our evolution as human beings. Without going into the technical details, suffice to say that the oldest parts of our brain are geared towards survival: fight and flight mode. Here, we are in a mode of fear, functioning instinctively. This part of the brain is continuously looking out for us, wanting to protect us from possible threats. It makes us believe that it is safeguarding us with its constant worrying thoughts and perceived dangers. While this is vital for our survival in some situations, we usually don't need it in the Western world for our everyday life. Yet, we have not unlearned to use this part. It kicks in all too often when not necessary. We all know how doubt can keep us from moving forward or taking a necessary next step.

In the past, it was vital for us to be able to mobilise all our physical strength in a critical situation, to run or fight. Today, in order to deal with the complex challenges of the world we live in, we need coherence of thought and emotions to react adequately. This is a new skill we can learn.

Our latest acquisition in our evolution as human beings is the prefrontal cortex. It is responsible for such things as the alphabet, music, science and creative thinking. According to Villoldo and Perlmutter ("Power up your brain. The neuroscience of enlightenment") this is where our future is located, and it is all about love.

Our upbringing has helped to wire our brain in a certain manner, but we can choose at any given time in our lives which part of the brain we wish to further develop, by using it and training it, rather like any muscle. Our neuronal networks are not fixed and can be changed and remodelled at any given time in our lives. Choosing to act out of love, rather than acting out of fear, we create new paths in our brains.

We actually rewire our brains by the choices we make every day, every instant of our lives. Science has shown that this can not only change our brains, but actually influence our genome for generations to come.

Think of it like different paths in nature. One is a trodden path which we've all gone down a million times and which we have been taught to use by observing our parents, teachers and society in general and generations before us. Then there are new paths, virgin territory.

Highly creative individuals, as well as those on a path to reconnecting with this full human potential, thrive on trying new paths, going down a different route. And we are even more creative and fulfilled if we do so coming from a place of love, compassion or any other form of love. This gives us access to our inexhaustible human potential, comparable to what mind-expanding drugs can do. More powerful because induced by ourselves without any outside help.

In light of the situation we are facing today on our planet, this is highly relevant. The skills and paths that have brought us to where the world is currently at, will not get us to a really new place. They have done their duty and need to be replaced or at least supplemented with new skills.

We, all of us, are pioneers, exploring unchartered ground. And one of the most essential forms of intelligence and energy that will support us on this path is creativity.

To better understand how this could work, let us look at our brains in more detail. Our memory is situated in the right part of the brain. This is where raw information, data, images, numbers and facts are stored, in fact any sensation without exception. However, in our everyday awareness, we only have access to the important data and sensations, thus only exploiting about one percent of this databank which we call memory.

The front left half of the brain, on the other hand, is the logical-analytical one. It controls the right side, filtering the raw material out of the unconscious, allowing only relevant information into the conscious realm of the brain. This prevents overstraining and allows us to function in everyday life.

The right side is the creative part of the brain which we activate by engaging in painting, music and other creative activities. Images also activate the information stored in our brains. By accessing this vast pool of data, we can obtain information and insights into a situation which by far exceed that of the analytical mind. This is very useful when we are confronted with having to make a decision or finding creative solutions. Both images and music can activate sources of energy that are not accessible through words alone.

We also access the data stored in our memory through relaxing. Outstanding inventions happen just this way. We have dealt in depth with all the data, facts, in other words all the necessary information that is therefore now stored in the brain. Then the moment of Eureka happens, when we go for a walk, when we are in a state of relaxation, no longer focusing on the actual problem consciously and our analytical mind has less hold on our vast data bank: creativity can now kick in.

Latest research on highly creative brains shows that they are more interconnected than those that have not been able to keep their genius alive into adulthood. In highly creative brains, areas that are not normally connected or that don't function together in other brains are actually working together.

"We found that the brain regions within the "high-creative" network belonged to three specific brain systems: the default, salience and executive networks. The default network is a set of brain regions that activate when people are engaged in spontaneous thinking, such as mind-wandering, daydreaming and imagining....The executive control network is a set of regions that activate when people need to focus or control their thought processes... The salience network is a set of regions that acts as a switching mechanism between the default and executive networks.

An interesting feature of these three networks is that they typically don't get activated at the same time. For example, when the executive network is activated, the default network is usually deactivated. Our results suggest that creative people are better able to co-activate brain networks that usually work separately." Roger Beaty

This constant flow of connecting in our heads can be absolutely exhausting and overwhelming and can lead to (mental) diseases. Our head alone is not equipped to deal with this, I believe.

In order to better manage what could otherwise easily get out of hand, and to allow for the flow of creative impulses in a more structured way, it is vital to join this process to the rest of who we are. To who we are in essence, our purpose or mission in life.

This will manifest itself through our other brains: the heart and the gut. When all three brains work together, we call this coherence.

Using simply one brain to channel our high and intense energy will feel like there is no on and off switch, an unfiltered effusion. Using all three brains helps us filter, sort and prioritise as well as find the most appropriate form to express and channel the creative energy at the present moment.

We will look at how to achieve coherence in more detail further down. For now, let us look at some simple ways to start creating coherence. When listening to certain types of music, and especially when playing music or singing ourselves, there is literally a firework of connections going off in our brains, as is visible in scans. The same is true for when we reach a peak doing sport, or in the flow of creating.

Another simple and powerful way to harmonise and synchronise our brain, is love. In a brain scan, scientists actually saw how love connects all the parts of our brain: back and front, right and left. We need to understand that love in this context is not necessarily romantic love, but the more embracing love which the Greeks called agape, as well as other forms of love, such as gratefulness, acceptance, appreciation and forgiveness. It is actually one of the most powerful tools we have to access our full creative energy. It involves our heart, the head and also the gut.

Through love - and this is what mystics of all ages talk about - we actually access the universe. This is where we become one. In modern terms, we connect to the Field.

Please take a moment right now to ponder the implications. This is very powerful stuff!

… to access the Field

To understand what happens when we are creatively inspired, when we have an insight or a gut feeling, let me challenge you with a radically new way of looking at this. One that we touched on earlier when talking about the Field. This will have a huge impact on realising how interconnected we really are with each other and the world we live in. Literally.

Looking at our world with these new eyes will enable us to believe in our powers of manifesting and creating on a whole new level. We will begin to see ourselves as creators, not only of certain works of art, projects or businesses, but literally of our reality and the world around us.

To this day, we believe that all our knowledge, memories and experiences are stored physically in our brains. As we have seen above, this would be in the right side of our brain. An entirely new approach, which I believe to make more sense, claims that the universal field of intelligence, called The Field, is a reservoir of knowledge, much like cloud computing technology that stores information. Everything is stored here. Our brains are then instruments with which we access this unlimited Field. This means we have access to data, to a kind of huge computer where all the knowledge and information humans have ever collected and thought and will ever think, is available. Intelligence and creativity would be an interaction with this enormous databank, using different parts of the brain, as well as our two other brains.

Could the Field offer a modern explanation to the questions: where do inspiration and intuition come from? Are we in constant contact with the Field, and are insights, inventions and creations a result of a dialogue and interactions with the Field? When invoking God or the Great Spirit, are we joining up with the infinite quantum Field of information?

Another new approach to intelligence, as opposed to the physically stored knowledge in specific parts of the brain, contends that intelligence has to do with connections in the brain: the more connections, the more intelligent we are. This finding is substantiated by medical research, whereby people who have lost the use of a part of their brain, can regain those skills by developing new connections in other places. Unlike what we have been told, these new connections can grow at any age, until we die.

As creativity establishes new connections by combining things in a different way, being creative is thus an act of intelligence!

If each brain is an instrument, a lens through which we gain access and information to the infinite Field, it is worth taking some time to understand what kind of a lens it is. To explore what each brain will enable us to achieve in our creative endeavours.

When do I want to focus on one brain rather than the other? And ultimately, how do I create coherence between all of them? What kind of information and knowledge will they filter for us? What exactly do we access with each of them? It is also a good idea, in the creative process, to evaluate which brain might be most helpful at the current moment and when we need coherence of all three. Let us then first look at each brain separately.

The head intelligence – insight

Our head is a powerful instrument for analysing, planning and "rationalising" things. The head is viewed as our intellectual brain, even though, as we have seen, it is a lot more. The rational part of the head is currently the most highly rated of all forms of intelligence in the West. People with a high IQ are venerated. It is only recently that emotional intelligence, and lately even spiritual intelligence, have begun to be of interest, as we realise that our rational capacities only take us so far. And we have also begun to see that people with a high IQ are often also highly sensitive and emotionally intelligent. The complexity of this topic goes beyond what we can describe here, but for practical purposes, let us still consider how best to use all the different forms of intelligence at our disposal, through the head, the heart and the gut. And for simplicity's sake I will talk about the heart as the seat of emotions and forms of love. Of the head as the analytical and planning intelligence and the gut as our instinctive, physical intelligence.

The intellectual mind is of course an integral part of anything we want to do or achieve, and has great value in planning, in understanding and structuring processes, making them manageable.

We can use the head a bit like a gate keeper. It can be useful to run new thoughts, insights and ways of thinking by this part of us, leading to new paths of action and new feelings. Rather like the parent of a teenager being the gatekeeper for safety: our "heads" make sure there is some sound evidence, some reasonable, good sense that keeps us grounded. It is a fine balance allowing the head into any creative endeavour, as it can easily kill our genius. Giving our head, the gatekeeper, the right nourishment in the form of thoughts to ponder, can open up its tight grip, the gateway, for us to enter new territory, and become radically more creative. We can then combine the old and the new. We do need our heads, as we need our wits about us. There are situations where the head is invaluable, let's not forget this.

Because the head is often the ruler in us, we need to take time to explore how our own minds work, i.e. how we approach things. What are our individual and personal thoughts on a topic? This is called the mindset. The mindset is one of the lenses through which we perceive reality. It is our focus and as such will inform the world we live in and which we co-create.

A creator's mindset will be different from that of a bookkeeper. It is also common knowledge that the mindset can be decisive in whether we are successful or not. It influences how we feel about a situation. If I think it's wrong to ever fail, it will certainly affect everything I do, and how I approach a project. If, however, I have learned that making mistakes is an integral, normal and even important part of creating anything new, I can actually start to explore my mistake as a guide to some hidden skill or new perspective. This will lead me to that untrodden path, where a hidden treasure is to be found.

Successful athletes use mindset techniques, involving visualising and imagining, to achieve victory. I first started working with some of these techniques in my musical career and found them to be really simple and effective tools for everyone. I now use them with business people to create new careers and businesses, as well as with creatives and artists, or clients on a healing path.

In channelling our creative energy, it is often our mind that will set the stage for success or failure. For whether we give up or pursue a new venture.

Putting a new mindset, a new approach into words, is rather like a form of modern mantra. In ancient India and still today, mantras were used as part of a spiritual practice, helping to focus the busy and wandering mind, leading to peace and, perhaps, enlightenment. For us, a new belief, formulated and spoken, is called an affirmation and can help us focus on what we wish to create.

A spoken sentence, though, is often not enough; it remains abstract, without any flesh, any impact. It needs to be associated with feelings and images. Let me illustrate.

A client lost her job. She was German and her visa was going to expire two and a half months after she was let go. She wanted to remain in Switzerland, as it was also the home base of her grown-up daughter who was studying abroad. When we started her programme, she was extremely stressed and under pressure. I also noticed that every time we got together she complained there weren't any jobs, nobody was calling back, she wasn't getting invited to interviews. After we had worked on her CV and cover letter, I felt I had to approach the subject: she was caught in an extremely negative spiral - understandably so. I suggested we do an exercise and she agreed, because she admitted to being in a negative space, feeling like a victim. In a guided inner journey, I led her to relax completely, go back to a time where she had been successful and achieved something outstanding. Then I asked her to fast forward into the near future and see herself succeeding with the same energy. There was more to this, but what I'm sharing here is that, thanks to a new frame of mind and believing it was possible, the next week when we got together, she had 3 interviews lined up. She managed to get a job in record time which enabled her to get her visa renewed and stay in Switzerland.

Using our minds in new ways has a profound and very practical effect on how we create. In spite of the findings of modern physics, most of us still live in an outdated model of the world where we perceive events with a linear approach of cause and effect: if I do this, it will lead to that. This is still very much engrained in our heads, and indeed our bodies and entire beings. And when we embark on a creative journey, we make plans, but then things turn out quite differently. With quantum physics, we now know that there can be non-linear evolution which cannot be "explained" in terms of cause and effect. We understand there are developments that go in leaps and jumps, a total shift of paradigm, a so-called "quantum leap".

Knowing this on an intellectual level can actually provide a context for us to experience being creative in a different way. In this case, the head, by learning about new ways of operating, can lead the way, allowing us to experience completely new processes.

This in turn opens the door to using our heads to connect to the inner pulse of life, to a higher form of wisdom through insight. Insights into a situation are extremely useful, motivating, and they help us embrace challenges, thus opening up a whole new dimension of creativity, flow and possibilities.

Insights are an important way to connect to a higher truth, something universal that is neither a feeling nor something to sense, but rather something to ponder. With ramifications. An insight can be ground-breaking, literally, and prepare the way for new emotional, practical and creative options moving forward. It clears the way for something entirely new, never conceived before. In this sense, an insight is a highly creative feat.

The heart intelligence: intuition

The heart is another lens through which we experience the world. When we are told to listen to our heart, this might be meant literally. We have finally come to understand that there is something we call "emotional intelligence" that is equally important as head intelligence. The heart senses connections where they are not obvious. It is usually concerned with the well-being of all involved. „Le coeur a ses raisons que la raison ne connait pas" - "The heart has its reasons that reason does not know"- is a common French saying. The heart can cause us to overcome barriers and to grow beyond our limitations.

As we saw earlier, a healthy heart does not beat absolutely regularly. There are endless, chaotic fluctuations and variations in a healthy heartbeat. Quite unlike any mechanical or electronically generated pulse. Imperfection and resilience, flexibility and adaptability are literally life-saving. A "perfect" mechanical heartbeat means death within a few days.

A healthy heart is one that varies its beat according to the situation we find ourselves in, one that adapts. It is flexible, and it is beating to the rhythm of our feelings.

There is a mutual interdependence between heart and mind: if I calm my heart, I calm my mind and vice-versa. It is not possible to be excited with a calm pulse.

We have talked about love, one of the most positive and strongest emotions we can feel. Activating this force could literally be life- saving. Did you know that you can actually die of a broken heart? Science has recently found that when we are in love, a certain part of the brain is very active. It is the same part that we activate when taking drugs, such as cocaine. It is our addiction centre. So, while we think of love as being situated in the heart, it is also connected to the brain in our heads. This supports the idea that opening our heart also opens our minds, enabling new thoughts, ideas and connections in our head-brain.

Activating forms of love, and especially self-love in our creative journey is, I believe, one of the most powerful sources of inspiration. It enables us to access parts of our creative potential we cannot reach through the head alone.

Unfortunately, it is probably also the greatest battle most creative people fight. Societal norms are strict. If we don't conform to them, we tend to be judged and we also judge ourselves for not being able to fit in, to achieve what is demanded of us. And this can be the greatest stumbling block in activating our full creative energy.

Loving myself is a rebellious act and an extremely powerful one!

Just like we can connect to our inner pulse on a higher, non-emotional level with the head, we can also do so with the heart. We will experience this as intuition. Intuition tells us something is right or wrong for us at that particular moment. We have a good feeling about something, or a mixed one. Here is powerful guidance to bringing who I am into the world.

My heart can be my guide, and loving who I am will enable it to function at its best. It's the fuel that drives my heart.

Learning to trust our intuition is perhaps one of the great challenges we face. You cannot rationalise intuition. There is no explanation, at least not on the level of facts and figures. If loving ourselves is one of the keys to unlocking our hidden potential, the heart is the instrument for this type of intelligence. It "knows" things that other parts of us don't.

When fear and the "head" are strong, this channel of receiving information can get distorted and we don't trust our intuition. Before any important decision, I have made it a point to sleep on it. That enables me to calm down, get into a state of coherence, and actually hear my own inner voice, my intuition, as well as my gut feeling. Then I'm best equipped to make a decision that is good for me on many levels, not just rationally.

The gut intelligence: impulse

Scientists have found our intestines, our enteric nervous system with bacteria and neurons, to represent another, even more important brain than the one in our heads. A lot of information and sensations would be stored here. I believe those that are not consciously accessible to us through the head. This could be where what psychologists call "repressed emotions" are stored. Emotions we haven't been able to deal with for many reasons: because they are too overwhelming, there has been trauma, events we cannot process or digest.

Our gut is the largest organ of immunity, it is extremely powerful. Some scientists actually speak of the gut as a "thinking organ" (Scheman). What is interesting is that head and gut have the identical cellular and molecular structure, so that medicine we use for our heads also works on the gut and vice-versa. Only recently have researchers found that more nerve cords go from the gut to the brain than the other way round. It appears that messages the gut sends to our head in the form of unease, nausea and pain are more important for our physical survival than vice-versa. When we take a decision, whether we are aware of it or not, we are always influenced by unconscious, stored emotions and by body reactions. We are informed by our gut feelings.

The wisdom of the gut exists, just like that of the heart. Chi-Gong exercises in Chinese medicine aim to balance and strengthen the Chi, our vital energy. The seat of the Chi is the belly, the centre of a person, according to Chinese philosophy. In martial arts this is where our concentrated power comes from. Could "acting from our gut" and breathing into our belly mean mobilising this energy?

The belly is our physical centre, the collective point of our physical energy and power. It is the seat of our instinct, a form of vital intelligence that we have in common with animals. Whereas animals generally seem to have no choice but to follow their instincts, we have our head brain that can prevent us from listening to our gut feelings, as well as our hearts that can stop us from acting on a gut feeling.

Gut feelings are by their very nature irrational. You cannot argue with them. If you try to rationalise them, they will disappear. As they don't have analytical and reasonable thoughts as their basis, but rather sub-conscious feelings and physical sensations, they are not accessible to the mind. This does not mean they are not valid. Any successful businessperson will attest to trusting her or his gut feelings to lead them to success. Even if they have to rationalise and find arguments for a decision once made in order to convince others, like shareholders or the board of directors.

We, in modern Western societies, are brought up to trust only what our heads can think, plan, conceive and document. If we stick to this form of intelligence, however, our scope of action is minimal.

Premonitions are a special form of gut feelings. Scientists made the following experiment: a computer displayed at random colour photos of relaxing scenes, i.e. nature or landscapes, or shocking and disturbing scenes, such as autopsies or erotic pictures. As was to be expected, the bodies of the participants relaxed immediately when they watched peaceful scenes and showed signs of agitation as soon as they saw erotic or repellent pictures.

But what is really significant in this context is that the researchers discovered the test person actually sensed what they were about to see. They registered physiological reactions before the respective photo appeared on the screen. The reaction was strongest before a repulsive picture, as if the person were trying to guard against it.

If gut feelings are related to instinct and survival, it can indeed be life-saving to trust them and to act on them, as I once experienced myself many years ago. I shared this dramatic story in my previous books: how standing on a platform I was compelled to step back just before a train rushed past me, and how this actually saved my life We all follow our gut instinct many times a day, often without even being aware of it. Here are some examples: sometimes you just know you need to turn off at a different place than what you see on the map; driving in the fast lane of a motorway, you know that a car in the slow lane is about to pull out and make you break; you sense that someone you just met is going to be trouble.

I suggest you begin noticing these irrational gut feelings. The more you do, the more you will be able to trust them. The gut is a vital organ in the creative process, because it's that intelligence that makes us move: stop, go somewhere, turn, speak – action in all kinds of form.

When we create, our gut is a special instrument of accessing the creative force. My head may be telling me something is not finished, needs more of this or that, but my gut feeling could be telling me to stop and let it be. This can be vital both for the project or piece I'm creating, and for my own inner balance and wellbeing.

Clearing, charging and rewiring our brains

The brains of highly creative people are constantly running high, always in action, forming new connections. This can be exhilarating and may in fact feel like being on a high, like others feel when they're on drugs. At the same time, to remain healthy and sane, this energy needs to be switched off from time to time.

Otherwise, we might end up having trouble sleeping and resting, which potentially could turn into a manic phase for those predisposed to this condition, or to burnout and other illnesses for others. We need to clear and empty our heads, our hearts and our guts, in order to recharge and rewire.

Emptying our brains is also necessary to create coherence, our highest form of intelligence. It's rather like emptying the garbage. If we don't, we get all cluttered up. For instance, take a situation, where you've been thinking a lot about an issue or a creative challenge, and you've gathered all the information you possibly can. Your thoughts are going round and round in your head. Your head is full. There is no room for anything new, for a new approach, insight or solution. Clearing your head will be the first necessary step in moving forward, to connect the wiring in your brain in such a novel way that it could bring the "Eureka" moment.

The same is true for emotions. We tend to not think of experienced emotions as being a hinderance or an obstacle in any way. I currently have a client who has experienced many traumatic occurrences in her life up to this day. She is full of these stored emotions. When a new situation arises that touches on the same topic, the trauma automatically gets triggered, and she has a hard time even conceiving that things might evolve differently this time. This is especially debilitating as her experiences concern just about every aspect of her professional life so far. Her extreme experiences are the basis for more of the same type, unless she "tidies up". Unfortunately, she is unable to see this at the present moment. Through no fault of her own she will keep recreating the same type of experience, which is heartbreaking to watch.

Equally, when a project we've put our all into fails, it can be quite emotional, in fact rather like losing someone we love. Before moving on with a new project, we will need to reflect and get clear on what happened, and in some way also feel the loss. It is important to understand and accept this, come to terms with the situation emotionally and mentally. Otherwise, emotions may block us from being a channel for new creative ideas. A negative experience can turn into a wall of fear, keeping us from ever trying again.

Once our brains are "empty" or in neutral, we can re-charge them and nourish them with positive energy: thoughts, feelings, insights, and movement, or a combination thereof. When we do this, we actually rewire our brains. It is important to understand that not only our heads, but all our brains, need to be cleared and re-charged, and that they never stop changing and evolving over the course of a lifetime.

Coherence: our brains co-operating

Commonly, the state whereby head and heart are in sync has been termed "coherence". I would like to extend this to include all of our brains: left and right part of the head, the heart and the gut. If all are aligned and functioning together, we as a whole function at a higher level, we are more satisfied, fulfilled and connected with the world around us.

Coherence is commonly defined as "Clarity of thought, speech and emotional composure" and as "The quality of being orderly, consistent and intelligible (e.g. a coherent sentence)." In terms of physics and waves/vibrations it is the "Synchronisation or entrainment between multiple waveforms. A constructive waveform produced by two or more waves that are phase- or frequency -locked."

To activate fully who we are, it is useful to look at our personal use of our three brains. We can actively take steps to create connections between them. We all know what it means if someone is incoherent due to pressure and anxiety: it is being unable to think straight and over-emotional. Coherence, on the other hand, enables access to flow and to expressing hitherto unused potential. Creating coherence between our brains means them communicating with each other, connecting and interacting, functioning as a whole, the sum greater than any or all parts. What does this mean in practical terms? How can we use it for creating something meaningful?

Let us begin by looking at how we normally function. In each of us, one brain or part of a brain is usually dominant, more active than the others. And this being the case, we need to understand that an intuitive person will perceive the same event or object in a different way from an analytical person.

We not only perceive the world through different lenses due to our upbringing, cultural background, skills and taste, we also live in our own personal world, depending on which brain we are most centred in. We differ in how we connect to the world around us, the Field, and consequently, what information we draw from there. We are, each one of us, intelligent in different ways, using different types of intelligence.

I personally believe this is what the modern term "neurodiversity" is all about. We have not understood this, because our Western world has been dominated by reason and the intellectual part of the head brain. And we have come to see humans as a kind of machine, where things always function the same way, in every one of us. Both our medical and our economical approach are based on this assumption. What's more, our Western "civilised " view of the world has spread across the globe.

Next time you argue with someone about what "really happened" or what is "really taking place", stop to remind yourself of this. It could well be that the other person is perceiving the same event with a different organ, through a different lens and therefore has different information about the situation. The only thing that makes sense is to share information you've perceived or received, and not argue about the nature of reality.

Let me illustrate how my different brains function for me, especially in challenging situations, because that's when our brains are the least coherent. When something stressful happens to me, I react with thoughts (head) and emotions (heart). I now understand why my reactions can be rather extreme: it is because my brain is so interconnected that it revs up to full potential to solve the problem. This is sometimes almost unbearable and can cause havoc, emotionally and physically, e.g. with a migraine or other symptoms. To relieve the pressure on my brain and emotions, I need to move into action, like walk around, call somebody to talk to, look up some information: I need to activate my gut brain to get into balance, into a state of coherence.

To really come to terms with a challenging event or situation in my life and find the most appropriate way to move forward, I will need to get all the facts I can, and also have some time alone. It's best for me to get moving somewhere in nature, to activate my gut feelings, my gut brain. I also need to sleep over any major decision I take. This helps me clear my head, connecting all the relevant parts of my brain, and it allows my feelings to flow more freely and thereby get an impulse for acting, for a next step.

Ultimately, I am using all three brains and getting them to interact, allowing for coherent thoughts, feelings and a course of action in keeping with what's best for me on all levels. Once I've synchronised my three brains, I can move on to the next step, perhaps something I need or want to do as a result of this. Or I may find peace through insight and acceptance.

The interaction of the brains is a subtle form of interplay and interconnectedness. There are as many variations on this theme as there are individuals. It is up to you to find the exact balancing points. To do so, observe yourself and get to know yourself in different situations.

Any creative process will benefit from your knowing how you are wired in your brains. You may find yourself more successful in the techniques you choose for activating your creativity and the type of channel you use for your artistic expression, as well as the best way forward when faced with an obstacle. Does it need to be physical as in movement, are you heart centred and therefore need to find something that touches your heart, a technique that allows your emotions to flow freely? Or do you like concepts and feel at home in organising or creating (artistic) concepts for yourself and others? The way you are centred in your brain(s) will ultimately need to be reflected in the way you present yourself to an audience or public, in marketing your creative endeavour or business.

Let me share, once again, a personal experience on my creative journey. After having produced 3 CDs with my own music, I had exhausted the electronic sounds of the medium I was using. Not knowing how to pursue, I started on a new route composing songs for piano and voice, nothing electronic. But here was the next challenge: although I have a nice voice, I didn't feel comfortable recording my owns songs with my own voice. Coming from a classical music background, my standards are extremely high, and my voice just doesn't seem good enough. It has taken roughly another 10 years before I'm courageous enough to even venture into this new territory. I'm finally beginning to explore how I could use my own voice for the songs I created 10 years ago. The path is creative once again: I'm playing with using my voice in a whole new way. And, most importantly, I understand now that I have to feel it. For me, because I was too focused on the technical (head) aspect, it never worked. Now I'm focusing on connecting with my heart and using my voice in a new way, by humming, being soft, moving with my body in flowing motion etc. And most importantly, feeling the connection to what I'm singing in my heart. I've actually begun the process of using my voice, not by singing my songs, but by finding and writing texts that move me deeply and just speaking them with my music rather than singing them. It feels right.

Understanding myself in how I function best, is the key. And by the way, this is an ongoing journey. So far, I've recorded some deeply moving texts by Khalil Gibran with my own music. I have also found inspiring and consoling words that I recorded with my music for a very close friend who finds herself in a challenging situation regarding her health. It has really helped her, I'm happy to say. Here is some of my deepest motivation to support and inspire someone I love.

There are a number of practices and processes all of us can use to create coherence of our brains and that have been proven to work. Whilst they basically work for everyone, as always, you will find your preference, what works best for you. Take the time you need to find out how you are centred, what brain you use in a preferred mode, and how to balance and synchronise all of them.

If we connect parts of our head brain with each other, and the head with heart and gut, this will create the highest degree of coherence.

I believe this to be the best way to channel our creative energy, because it is using all of our inherent potential, allowing all aspects of ourselves to cooperate with each other. This also gives us access to a new level of intelligence that will bring our world into a new dimension, both for us as humans and for the entire planet.

This is our personal journey as well as our collective human journey into a new era.

CO-OPERATING WITH THE CREATIVE ENERGY

Many of the challenges we face, whether effectively using our exiting highly creative resources or on the way to becoming a highly creative person, can be better managed when we accept ourselves for who we are, when we love our unique gifts and cooperate with this energy.

Again, as no two creative people are alike, this is a personal process of finding what works best. This may also change over the course of a lifetime. When you accept yourself as you are and life the way it is, you begin to co-operate with the universe.

Your best starting point for whatever you're trying to create -supportive relationships, a meaningful job, good health or a work of art - is right where you are at that very moment in your life, just the way it is. Accepting life, a situation and your starting point is the first step to cooperating with your creative energy. This mobilises most of your creative potential, as you don't waste energy on dreaming of perfect conditions or fighting what is not perfect at that particular moment.

Accepting life as it is at a given moment and using it as a starting point, is what I call co-creating with life. Co-creating is like stepping into a river of creative energy which we can navigate to some extent, although the river will also have its own direction and challenges, affecting the route we take. As we have seen in the loopholes of creativity, we will always need to allow for the unexpected which is life or the creative intelligence entering into the creative process. If not, we cut ourselves off from a huge reservoir of possible options and from some greater form of intelligence. We can plan our creative project to some extent, yet there are aspects that are unpredictable. This is why I don't believe in visualising and imagining all the exact details of an outcome, unless you're 100% sure you know exactly what it is you want and what it should look like. I would recommend, when visualising, that you imagine the feeling of the outcome, and with it perhaps a gesture or feeling of accomplishment such as a congratulatory handshake, the applause of the audience, or the deep satisfaction that comes with the result. Focus on this rather than the details of how to get there.

Why? Because when we imagine anything, we do so based on our experience up to date. This is our greatest obstacle to creating something beyond our wildest dreams, something better than what we've ever experienced in our lives so far. Not knowing what the desired outcome feels like in our bodies, emotionally and in our minds, makes it almost impossible to create that very thing.

So how do we visualise the best possible outcome?

We can either base it on an experience we've had: any small step that went in the right direction and that made us feel good. Or we daydream ourselves into another person's life, a real person or one in a film, thus imagining what it could feel like. Either way we need to connect in some way to something beyond ourselves and our current situation.

Pick one single moment in time where you had a glimpse of what you wish to create and expand on that. That glimpse into another reality will be your entry into another world.

Growing up in different countries and cultures, I never had an experience of belonging, of feeling myself to be part of a community. Due to this, as well as feeling misunderstood as a result of being highly gifted and creative, I've felt very lonely many times in my life. Imagining this to be different was rather like trying to pull myself out of quick-sand – an impossible task. The only way I've been able to do so has been step by step, always acknowledging the tiniest steps in the right direction. These steps can be so seemingly insignificant that we can easily overlook them and don't believe the desired result to be possible. It has taken me a good twenty years to create a feeling of belonging, but I can imagine a lot more yet to come.

A vital aspect of creating beyond what we're able to imagine is noticing progress, registering new elements, perceiving the slightest change. This is actually where many people fail. They believe progress has to be in milestones, in end results, how we imagined it. If it doesn't manifest this way in our lives, we tend to overlook it, it doesn't seem valid and therefore we miss this vital stepping stone.

Generally speaking, I've noticed in my own and in my clients' lives that progress tends to be slow at the beginning, almost unnoticeable, but once we've reached a critical point, things begin to move faster. Also, when we next create something new and different, we've become more confident in our powers of manifestation, and that allows for faster progress as well.

Planting the seed of intention

As we know from nature, every living being on earth is created from a seed. Our creative projects are also initiated through a seed, the seed of intention.

More than ten years ago I joked that when hybrid cars would be sold second hand, I would buy one. I even knew which one, but at the time they were too expensive for me. I completely forgot about this. Last year this seed became a reality. I now own a hybrid car. Not because I thought about it for ten years, it was only because my sister bought one first, and that made me think about buying one as well. It materialised, and then I realised I had planted this seed ten years ago.

Another seed of intention I planted in my life, was wanting to compose music in my very own way. I explored all the possible options at the time. Because I wanted to be able to record what I improvised, and then be able to translate this music into sheet music, there was a technical aspect involved: I needed the right device with the right technology. At the time I was imagining this, it didn't exist. Ten years later, I was able to take the first step by exploring all the devices that existed: synthesizers, keyboards and e-pianos. All of these are able to do this, even if still not really in a satisfactory way. It was a gigantic step in my process of composing on my own terms. This seed had grown up and come to fruition.

Once the seed is in the soil and you've given it your all, but there is no progress, it's time to allow nature, or in our case, life to take its course. From time to time, we make sure there's nothing more we can do, or we take another step to materialise our intention. Suddenly the seed has grown and we can see a first tentative little plant above ground. This may be the time to take it one step further. And so on. It is the intention and the focus that will bring the seed to fruition.

Focusing on the desired result

When teaching beginners to play the flute, what often happened was that they tried so hard to produce a sound - unlike a piano or a guitar you have to produce the sound through the way you purse your lips, and blow against the edge of the flute at a certain angle - that they were unable to play a piece rhythmically and in time.

I developed a technique whereby I had my students feel the inner pulse of the music, like a heartbeat that beats on and on, one they could feel inside, regardless of what they were playing. Learning to focus on that, rather than the actual sound and the rhythm, made them stay in that musical flow, in the energy of the entire phrase. What happened then was miraculous: they were able to play in time with the correct rhythm and with a proper sound!

Translated into how we use language, this can be likened to thinking in whole sentences, as opposed to individual words.

This is a key principle of creation: focusing on the larger pulse, on the essence, can allow the details to come together in the perfect manner. Life will take care of the details if we focus on the essence. The intention and focus on the pulse allow the rest to unfold. In this case, the inner pulse of the music is the focused intention. Just acting as if, somehow liberates the energy so it can follow the intention.

Much later, reading about quantum physics and about the fact that energy follows the focus, I had the theoretical backup for this. It's as if the big wave of intention carries the small waves of coordinating sound and rhythm. Meaning, not individual words, structures the sentence.

If my intention is strong enough, the details will follow.

Connecting to the inner pulse of
life through inspiration

Inspiration is a way to connect to that greater intelligence, to life, thereby enabling us to cooperate and co-create. Inspiration not only connects us with the inner pulse of life, it also connects all our brains with each other. This happens to some degree involuntarily and cannot be forced. We can, however, prepare the ground for it, as it comes when we empty ourselves and open up, making room for it. A full glass has no space for more liquid.

In order to create coherently and in keeping with who you are, it is so important to know what inspires you. This will reveal a great deal about your essence and what matters to you and will also allow you to connect to your life and purpose.

Imagine the wind playing its tune through reeds or bamboo. Inspiration is like the universe playing through you. It brings your essence alive, making it sing. If you allow it to do so, if you are in resonance with the gentleness, the strength and the direction of the energy, who you are at heart is reinforced and you can create the most beautiful sounds and unique melodies. It is as if you were connecting your individual pulse to the greater pulse of life.

Inspiration is not fixed for an entire life, but there will most probably be an underlying theme for everything that inspires you over the course of your life. Just like when we love, we need to go searching for it and choose to focus on it time and again. It can easily get lost in our day-to-day activities and demands.

Tune into what inspires you and cultivate it.
Look at the people who have inspired you in your life and perhaps still do:

- *Who are they and what do they stand for?*
- *What feelings do they invoke?*
- *What action would you take if you were like them?*
- *How would you lead your life?*

Buddhism and different forms of meditation showed me a way of dissociating myself from everyday life, from ambitions and other attachments. They enabled me to release and clear my brains. However, they also left a void. It seemed like a first and necessary step in connecting to some larger force and intelligence, but did not leave me where I really wanted to be. The counterpart for emptying ourselves is filling up with something greater. This transpersonal energy flows through us in the form of love, compassion, wisdom and inspiration.

Using inspiration to connect to the Field, the pulse of life or God, if you like, potentially means being at home everywhere and at any given time.

Doctors, especially in the UK, are prescribing museums of art, music, dancing, meditating and spending time in nature. Why? Because all the minor and major ailments of modern society, with depression and burnout at the top, are costing our health system and our economy horrendous amounts of money. And research has finally proven what common sense and experience have been telling us all along: that these are sustainable, easy to apply, and very cost-effective ways of raising the level of wellbeing in our individual lives, and society in general.

There are of course many reasons for this. One of them which we will highlight here is that they are spaces for inspiration. We step outside of our daily hustle and bustle. The mind becomes quiet and focused on something deeper and larger than daily life and our to do list. We connect with our essence and the essence of being human.

Art, music, creative expression and nature are essential to our survival, to feeling well balanced, grounded and at home on Earth.

When we are inspired, this allows us to create from a larger source, granting meaning not just for ourselves, but also for others. This source provides us with an inexhaustible energy.

Inspiration comes in many different forms: through images and visions, through words and sounds, thoughts or feelings, and sensations that run through our entire bodies and minds. Let us then explore these different forms. Remember, there is not one way for everyone. Find that which most resonates with you and explore how inspiration wants to come through you. Perhaps you didn't even know that it was inspiration knocking at your door. Inspiration most often urges us to express it and share it. We wish to inspire others. Like love when it is shared, inspiration multiplies and elevates us. That is inspiration at its best.

As a form of coherence, inspiration touches our mind with insight, our heart with forms of love and wisdom, and our gut by the way it wants us to express.

Ask yourself this:

- *Do I receive inspiration through seeing something: through perceiving the beauty of something or watching somebody do something?*
- *Or through hearing something: music, voice, sounds of nature or somebody talking?*
- *Or is it through movement of some sort: dancing, climbing, acting, pantomime or other physical expressions?*
- *Through reading or hearing wise, beautiful words?*
- *Am I inspired by deeds, by how people act, what they do or how they do it?*

Accordingly seek out inspiration through the sense that speaks to you most directly. Because images have become such a predominant expression of our world, I will go into this sense in more detail, having explored many of its hidden aspects in my art.

Images and visions: receiving information and inspiration from the Field

When talking about visions and images, it can be useful to first look at how our perception depends on our inner focus, our attitude. It is influenced by ideas and thoughts we have formed, leading to a certain perspective on things, as well as to creating certain visions for ourselves. Indeed, what happens inside of us is perhaps even more relevant than what we see in the external world in the form of images.

A vision is a series of images that we see with our inner eyes. This is one of the tools in the creation process that can act as a powerful guide, connecting us with our innermost essence and feeding us along the way. It is definitely worthwhile looking into what vision you have for yourself, your life and perhaps the world we live in. This will act as a powerful benchmark and keep you on track when creating. It can be an endless source of inspiration.

A perspective, our inner focus, is the lens through which we look at a situation. We can choose to change our perspective on something or someone, and thereby enable another vision, and ultimately reality. What if we opted to regard our current situation from a perspective of it being perfect - not in an absolute sense. Not having enough money is, of course, by no means a perfect situation. But perhaps it is the perfect situation to motivate us to take necessary steps to a more fulfilling life or to begin monetising a creative endeavour, simply because we need to.

I suggest we look at our current situation in life as being the perfect starting point for whatever it is we wish to create. Perfect from another, higher perspective. One we need to grow into at times, that is not necessarily obvious on the surface, that may be hidden. Let us then try to find that perspective that will enable us to perceive it this way. We will need to be willing to not be right and have all the answers, to let go of resentment or hurt or anger, as much as we also need a profound trust in life and the universe we live in.

This book is as much about expressing our individual creative essence as it is about manifesting and creating our future world together. And this way of looking at the world is certainly challenging when we look at the state it is currently in. Luckily, it is possible to create our own environment of peace, beauty and trust in the midst of a troubled world. In so doing, we will automatically create a haven and anchor for others, a vital building block for a new world. Remember, we are all and everything connected with all there is. This connection exists, regardless of whether I focus on it consciously or not. We will automatically, through our connection in the Field, connect with others on the same path, whether in person, virtually, or just in spirit. This can help put our minds at peace, knowing we are not alone.

Besides visions and perspective, I would also like to include stories here. They are perhaps the most powerful series of images, because they come from within. We create and choose the images we see inside ourselves when listening to a story. This is true for stories we are told by others, as much as our own stories we tell ourselves.

Let us now turn to images in the outside world, remembering they always connect with our inner images, triggering meaning and inspiration based on who we are.

An image can be used as a guide, for orientation, inspiration and as a source of information. Images allow us to see the larger picture and to change perspective. They are highly effective tools for visualising what we wish to create.

We have seen how the right side of our brain is the creative part which we activate by engaging in painting, music and other artistic activities. Images also activate all the information stored in this part of our brains. Through images we get access to data stored here and can thus obtain information about a situation, exceeding by far that of the conscious mind. This is very useful when we are confronted with having to make a decision or finding creative solutions.

Images access intelligence in a much more fundamental and wholistic way than words or ideas can. They provide an abundance of information that cannot be accessed through our rational minds. Modern science actually contends that intelligence works in images. So, it's worth decoding this form of knowledge and wisdom.

Both inner images and pictures we encounter in the outer world speak to archaic layers of our consciousness, where they unfold their impact. The fact that images can store an abundance of information is used to memorise many more facts than we could otherwise remember.

According to neuroscientists, we are normally able to memorise only five characteristics or facts at a time. Memory trainers use images and stories to remember an endless row of facts.

Utilising images as sources of information and of inspiration, we can explore our personal images regarding a topic, a question or a problem. In an act of high creativity, we can create images that represent complex situations, inspire us, guide us and remind us of deep truths. When painting, drawing, taking a photo or doing a collage, we can let our inner wisdom guide us, allow a colour, a sense of beauty or a compelling shape lead the way to a deep truth and to our essence.

In a next step we can learn to decode their multi-dimensional message. We need to keep in mind that pictures are tools and messengers, not absolute truths. The meanings of images are not fixed, and need to be understood from the context, somewhat like in the Chinese language where a complex sign can change its meaning depending on its position and surrounding additional signs.

What we can distinguish is the type of picture we are dealing with. Is it figurative or abstract? Put simply, figurative pictures represent people, animals, buildings, landscapes, objects and anything that physically exists in our world. A geometrical figure, simple lines or shapes which do not represent anything in a concrete, physical way, would then be abstract. Abstract pictures can only be interpreted symbolically, figurative ones either symbolically or concretely.

I would like you to experiment with the effect pictures can have on you. Bear in mind that our physical bodies and our minds, our systems cannot distinguish between seeing real pictures and imagined ones. Both have the same effect on us.

Simply imagining something has a tremendous effect, a fact we can utilise to create either wellbeing or anxiety.

Timing, rhythms and cycles

Timing is decisive for substantiating any idea. Many creative endeavours fail because we don't understand this element of creation. Factoring time into the equation when creating connects us directly with some greater intelligence.

Timing is a key factor in co-creating life and, in fact, in creating anything at all. If something just won't move forward or isn't happening, there may be a reason for it. It may not be the right time. Or perhaps there is a missing element in your plan, a skill not yet mastered. Synchronising our individual pulse to the universal pulse, as well as that of what it is we wish to create, is crucial in order to reach our goals and lead a happy life.

Every moment in time has a certain quality. In the Bible, Ecclesiastes 3, there is a well-known text which describes how for every enterprise and each event there is a right time: birth and death, losing and finding, even for loving and hating, war and peace, just like wailing and dancing. It is also written there that we can only do so much. God – in modern terms universal intelligence or life - will take care of the rest, with the whole, with everybody's interest in mind. It is actually describing our inner pulse and that of the universe.

In my own life, time always seems to play a crucial role. Much of what I wanted, wished for and planned, did not work out and materialise immediately. Sometimes it took months, other times decades. Being at odds with this cost me a lot of energy, but seems to be a necessary process in being able to let go.

Besides the right, or should I say, the fitting moment for what you wish to create, there are general cycles and rhythms. There is the rhythm of day and night, the yearly cycle with its seasons, the duration of a life and many more. Our achievement-orientated society has completely lost sense of this, as it has lost touch with anything that is natural. In modern culture, the general work ethic wants us to work more and longer hours, and always at a faster pace, constantly pushing us to achieve more. We don't allow for pauses and rest. However, inhaling and exhaling is important not just for our bodies and for all of our brains, but also for our mind. After inhaling, we need to exhale.

In nature, active phases are followed by periods of rest. I find this especially impressive with hibernating bears. But plants also wither, die in autumn and sprout in spring. They are seemingly dead, but continue to live underground, kind of dozing, gathering new strength in the dark womb of the earth.

Rhythms go from out to in, active to passive, up and down and back again. Many people have lost the connection to these rhythms which are not only intrinsically connected to nature, but also to the "above" and "below" part of human existence: the spiritual, higher, universal aspect is overruled by the earthly, practical, material and ego-centric.

I learned that for me, as a highly creative person, waiting and being passive and receptive are essential phases, because these states connect me with the greater pulse of life. They allow for ideas and creative processes to gestate and get nourished in many different ways they wouldn't otherwise. I also believe that these states are antipodes, wanting to be experienced. They have something to do with the female aspect of our human existence. You could call it the natural aspect in an otherwise technologically orientated world where everything seems feasible, if not always sensible or desirable.

The receptive moments are those where we connect to ideas, insights and impulses, as well as where we become that reed through which the wind blows... for inspired creation.

In my life I try to recognise rhythms and cycles, even if I have to admit that periods of passiveness, darkness and unclarity are sometimes hard to manage and accept. Understanding them as a vital part of any creative process, like a seed germinating, takes away the suffering and self-blaming.

Another crucial aspect of timing is the way we structure our own time, over the course of a day, week or year. It is vital to make time to create, to receive inspiration and to connect to the larger picture. Of our lives or what we are creating. This is true for everyone:

whether you are already living a highly creative life or just setting out on this journey. Otherwise, we can easily get caught up with daily chores and things we have to do, pushing the creating time to the back, neglecting what is vital for our health and wellbeing. If we don't make time to create on a regular basis, life may well force us to: we get ill, lose our jobs, get divorced...

Find out which time of the day is your most creative time:

- *Are you a morning person or a night owl?*
- *When does creative expression flow most naturally?*
- *When do you feel most inspired?*

And then block out at least an hour at that time, even if it means getting up earlier, not meeting friends in the evenings, or staying in for lunch. You will notice immediately how much better you feel if you do this. And don't stop when things get challenging or when things are running smoothly. Keep that undercurrent of your life flowing, even if you're not in the middle of an inspiring project: at your designated time do some research, brainstorm new ideas, go for a walk, go to places that inspire you, or simply relax and allow your soul to roam freely...

This structure can be one of the most vital elements to giving your creativity a form, to expressing it in the material world and to seeing a physical result, and perhaps even reaping some financial benefits from it. Keep going, always. And if one day or one week you can't, for whatever reason, make sure you get back to this "routine" as soon as you can. The longer you have been integrating this kind of routine into your life, the easier it will be to return to it. Remember also to stay flexible as to its outer form: maybe the time will change over the course of your life, maybe the place will be different.

It is about giving that inner flow of the creative energy a designated space in your life.

Connecting to the mysterious inner pulse of creation

A very special way of creating is connecting to the inner pulse of our creative project. If we understand that in The Field everything is connected to everything else, that everything and every being vibrates at a certain frequency, we can understand that it is possible to communicate with just about anything. We can tune in and resonate with, basically, any other pulse out there. This means we can tune into a project, a work of art or creative endeavour, and communicate with it as we would with a living being.

You may wonder how we could possibly do that. Ancient shamans and healers had no problem with this. They went into a state of trance to communicate with plants and animals for healing, but also with the sick part of a person, and their soul. It is in our genetic heritage to do so. What has changed is our belief about the world we live in and how it functions. We no longer believe this to be possible, let alone desirable or useful. This is, once again, where the lens I chose to look through will determine how I experience reality.

You do not need a specific technique, but there are certain things that favour an exchange with the universal Field. Going into those sacred spaces in which external sensory stimuli or physical activity are reduced, allows for a kind of connecting inward. It is also vital to trust that it can really work. What will definitely support this form of communication is a strong desire to communicate - a personal motivation is the strongest enabler. Opening up to this inner process that cannot be entirely controlled is as if you were trusting yourself to the current of a river without knowing where it will take you.

Connecting to the inner pulse of what we are creating can be very helpful in trying to get more and different information from what we know with our conscious minds, from what is apparent and obvious.

Highly creative individuals, and also professional oracles, have this ability to see behind what is obvious. Interestingly enough, this is usually perceived as a spiritual gift, rather than being connected to creativity. Highly creative persons recognise patterns, see connections where others don't. What's more, they can actually see into other dimensions, as I have described in accessing other states of consciousness. They have the capacity to tune into these fields, into the vibes of a place, into the pulse of an event. Whereas oracles do this for counselling, shamans use this technique both for healing and to see determining energies of a situation that are not immediately obvious.

We, as highly creative individuals, can do this to create, to channel inspiration from universal intelligence, and to get guidance about what wants to be birthed into the world through us. Like with any skill, it takes openness, receptivity and practice.

You will need to learn about different states of consciousness: in an active mode, it will be difficult to receive accurate information. Rather like a full glass that has no room for more. So being able to go into alpha or even deeper states of relaxation, induced by meditation and various relaxation techniques, can be a first step. The creative state of flow is another one. Here, it is more like channelling the energy into a form and connecting to our essence, allowing us to feel that deep connection to our life and purpose.

The power of thoughts, words and sound to create

Many indigenous people, amongst them the Aborigines and the Native Americans, believe that rocks and mountains are alive and that animals and plants have a soul. They also believe that we create beings and elements of nature by naming them. The Genesis of our Bible states that in the beginning was the word, and the word was God. Virtually, by naming something, perceiving and recognising it, we create it. Might this be a parallel to the perception of a quantum particle?

When we talk about creating something, most of us would probably think in terms of creating artistically, manually or conceptually. But how about what we create verbally and in our mundane everyday thinking? Are we always aware of this powerful tool of creation? Our thoughts and words are like the blueprint of anything we want to manifest. They will enable certain things and not others. Like a mould that matter flows into to help spirit take shape.

When we tell others about what we're doing we are in fact manifesting our creation with sound.

When we consult psychologists, counsellors or doctors, whether alternative or traditional, Western or Eastern, spiritual or hands on, they all have an impact on how we perceive ourselves and how we evolve to become whole and strong. What they say, their tone of voice, their message and the way they tell us, all have an effect on our success or failures, our wellbeing and what we believe possible for ourselves. What any kind of consultant, or person we know for that matter, says about who we are and what we do, has a huge impact.

Because this is so, I am very careful of what I say when coaching and advising people. I share with them the belief that anything that is really essential to them will be possible in some way, although we may not have control over the actual outcome and timing.

A Chief Human Resources Officer of a global luxury hotel chain lost his job. One thing he was really keen to explore was setting up his own business. At the same time, he was used to earning a very high regular income and had issues with insecurity. I was convinced he had what it takes because of various factors regarding his career and personality. So, I created the space for him to develop to the point where he could feel it himself. It was a step-by-step process during which I guided him to be brave, define his services, and also use everything he had at his disposal, including his network. After a few months, he let go of wanting to find a job and fully embraced his new business - a success story. Every time he had come to our sessions, unsure, doubting, feeling low, I encouraged him and said I believed in him.

Creating has a lot to do with beliefs and visions we hold for ourselves. They are the parameters within which we create. These in turn are influenced by what we and others think about ourselves and our lives, as well as about how our world functions.

Self-fulfilling prophecies do exist.

Often, we are not even aware of our beliefs because they have become so much a part of who we think we are. And also, a part of our collective consciousness, what we humans believe in a certain culture at a designated moment in time. They will be like the proverbial pink elephant, the one we try not to think of. And it takes discipline to focus on what we really desire in our minds and hearts. Luckily, we do not depend on anyone outside ourselves. We have the power to choose what we want to talk about, what we want to believe and what thoughts we want to cherish. We select what is best for us, and how we do it. We have the choice to connect with those people who will support our own narrative.

As a highly creative person who has outed yourself, you will come into contact with many views on you as a person and on who you are. How many times was I told that I was so lucky to be highly creative, and why was I even worrying or lamenting? Not being understood made me feel like I was wrong, and that I should be like everyone else. I was the problem.

We all take what we hear seriously, it affects our subconscious mind, even if we dismiss it consciously. And this is especially true, when we are seeking guidance, because we tend to give the counsellor power over the matter we're consulting on, and possibly even over ourselves. This is probably one of the reasons some people don't like to consult anyone, whether fortune-tellers or doctors, because they're afraid of what they're going to hear, and how it's going to affect them. And rightly so!

We can use words to build or destroy, to empower or weaken. We can use words to get across who we are, what we do and how we do it. This is as important when talking to others as it is when we talk to ourselves, in our thoughts. Stories are thoughts and ideas manifested. The wisdom of ancient ages was passed on to future generations through stories, not technical explanations nor a list of ideas.

Ask yourself this:

- *What story am I telling myself about my current situation?*
- *What am I telling others?*
- *Can I rewrite the story so that it gives me strength, faith and courage to create what really matters to me?*

Voicing our calling, birthing it into the world

An important aspect of words is their sound. As we have seen, the world, according to many myths, was created through word-sound. The use of our voice as an instrument of creation is certainly worth exploring. I have actually helped people get a job by enabling them to use their voice in a manner more suited to their purpose and job.

A client once contacted me to help him in the application process. He was getting invited to interviews and then didn't get any further. The feedback was that he didn't come across as being confident enough. He's a lawyer.

So, to help build his confidence, we worked on the wording of his answers to interview questions, and on understanding his strengths. During this process it became increasingly clear to me that we would need to work on his voice. It was rather high pitched and slightly broken and, no matter what he said, in this tone of voice he would not come across as being confident and strong. The first and greatest challenge was for him to hear this. Then I gave him some simple exercises to connect with another part of his voice, the deeper one. He practised and got the job he wanted. We didn't change who he was, we just made it possible for another part of him that was somewhat hidden and unexpressed, to come forth and be heard.

Our voice is a very powerful instrument of creation and it's connected to who we are in our very essence.

Vocation and voice have the same latin stem: vocare = to call. Our voice is connected to our calling.

When we listen to other people's voices, we respond to their sound, whether we want to or not. There are those voices that are pleasant, that resonate within us, and those that push us away and make us uneasy. By the same token, our own voice reflects hidden aspects of ourselves.

There are within us different voices which we can use for different purposes. All of this is well worth exploring. Suffice to say that, as we explore who we are, our voice plays a significant part and can support us in creating what we want. Certainly, voicing and expressing who we are and what we wish to create, play a central role in the creative process. As much as listening to our inner voice of wisdom, intuition and insight.

True magic: the pulse of things and we are one

As we have seen, there is a mysterious inner pulse to anything we create. And there's an inner sense of timing that comes with it, as well as an external pulse that we encounter in visible growth, signs and events in the outer world. When both pulses, our inner and the outer one, resonate in sync we call this synchronicity. This is experienced as coincidence or fate – depending on the nature of the event, and on our beliefs.

When we express our inner voice in the outer world, our own pulse meets with the outer pulse of life, of the universe around us. When both come together, beating

to a common larger beat, we experience this as true magic.
We feel connected, in flow, in tune, supported and loved.
This pulse can carry us beyond anything we've ever
imagined, beyond our wildest dreams.

*Together, I and universal intelligence, are more than
I could ever be on my own.*

The pulse of things and we are one

Can you hear it,
the breath of water?
Can you hear them,
clouds floating by?
Can you hear
the songs of your soul?
Hear it, see it, touch it...
the pulse of things as they unfold.
The pulse of things and we are one.

Can you see it,
the sound of snow?
Can you see them,
stones growing old?
Can you see
the beauty of your soul?

Hear it, see it, touch it...
the pulse of things as they unfold.
The pulse of things and we are one.

Can you touch them,
the words we spoke?
Can you touch them,
our hidden thoughts?
Can you touch
love at its core?

Hear it, see it, touch it...
the pulse of things as they unfold.
The pulse of things and we are one.

© Tessa Richter, 2013

THE CREATIVE MINDSET

The term mindset is being used more and more frequently. But what does it actually mean?

Our mindset is the set of beliefs we have that form the lens through which we perceive reality and the world around us. It is the way our mind works in dealing with our reality. It is a habitual or characteristic mental attitude that determines how we interpret and respond to situations, and is very much influenced by our upbringing, our parents and the environment we grow up in. It is a determining factor in how we deal with what life presents us with, and how we achieve and reach our goals. Much research is currently being done on how it also affects our ability to heal.

A mindset can favour success or failure, healing or getting sick. Luckily, as beings who are conscious of ourselves, we can observe our mindset and, if desired, develop a new mindset adapted to our circumstances and the challenges we are facing. One that reflects who we truly are, in the present moment, and which ultimately serves us better. This is a conscious choice we have.

Viktor Frankl, a survivor of the Holocaust, is an expert on the topic of conscious choice. He wrote about the fact that we have a choice in how we view and deal with challenging situations. And a mindset expert I listened to a while ago, told the story of how he was diagnosed with pancreatic cancer with a death rate of 95% within 3 years. The decisive moment and huge mind-shift that enabled him to still be alive 10 years later happened when he realised that 5% actually survive. From then on, he focused entirely on being part of the 5% and he set himself a positive goal of doing a triathlon after the chemotherapy. He started his training while still on chemo.

I have written this book for you, Highly Creative Person, but also for all of us humans who share the gift of creative genius, to understand what a mindset could look like that serves our huge creative energy and potential. It is by understanding the creative process, timing, one's own approach and purpose related to this topic, and all of the other topics covered in this book, that we can begin to build a mindset suited to a creative person's life.

The mindset is what makes things possible. By cultivating a highly creative person's mindset you are paving the way for this powerful current to flow through you into the world. You will be able to express all those unique and inspiring creations waiting to be channelled by you - and you only!

One of the most important and decisive factors in creating what matters to you that we haven't yet talked about, is patience and perseverance. As we have seen in the chapter on timing, things sometimes take a lot longer than we have learned to believe. Those people who don't give up when they don't have immediate results, or the results they've created don't satisfy them, are most likely to ultimately create meaning, wellbeing and what matters to them in their lives – whether it be a career as an artist, setting up one's own business, achieving better health or fulfilling relationships.

At the threshold of a new dawn of humanity, where AI and digitalisation are at the forefront, we also have the power to create a world based on kindness and cooperation. Let' s not give up too soon, even when things seem to be going into the diametrically opposite direction.

When we visualise a desired outcome, it is essential to look at what is holding us back, what obstacles we need to overcome. Not factoring this in can definitely mean unrealistic expectations and will cause us to give up prematurely.

Using the earlier example of the Chief Human Resources Officer, the obstacles were no experience, uncertainty and the wish for a stable income – all aspects we addressed in the coaching process and took care of one by one: if you want to set up your own business, you will need a sellable product and potential customers. Then you need to create marketing materials and a strategy to implement the business and earn money. In our case, he was already doing some mindfulness programmes for the employees, and that was the first product he could build on. His experience as a CHRO was the second line of products. By coming up with ideas to whom to sell these respective services, he began building his clientele and realised there was indeed a market. In turn, this allowed him to believe that the plan was actually feasible.

Try to be patient and kind with yourself and the world we live in when things don't materialise in the desired way. Rather like a parent's attitude toward their child. Love, care and persistence.

Dare to create now!

We have looked at the creative process and forces at work that contribute and influence it, and we have delved into the nature of the creative life force. Hopefully, by now you are ready to create and express this energy! Perhaps you're already a creator? Or you've always felt like you'd love to write, paint, build, cook, create something unique? Or are you one of the building creators of our future as mankind?

Understanding that you are a unique instrument through which the universe creates will have hopefully enabled you to feel how important your creation is. Even if there are millions of other people out there doing something similar, only you can bring YOU and your essence into the world. You are an absolutely unique instrument of creation. No one, and I mean no one, can do what you do!

If creativity is powerful, it is also neutral. As we have seen, the creative force does not discriminate and it can come uninvited with uncontrollable timing, through crises or inner urges. Sometimes the flow of ideas, insights, emotions wanting to be expressed is confusing and so overwhelming we give up altogether, unable to find the most appropriate outlet and expression at that precise moment in time. The energy is such that we want to do it all at once. Structure and co-creating with life as it is are two powerful guides helping us to streamline and ground us.

Besides these practical guiding principles, I have found a triad that will help you to know what wants to be birthed into the world through you at this present moment:

know yourself – love who you are and create what matters

Knowing yourself is understanding what kind of unique instrument of creation you are. It is so-to-speak your wiring. Loving who you are is the energy, the current that will bring the wiring to life, activating your potential. And creating what matters is using this energy to express your purpose in the world. One feeds the other, and all three are integral parts of the creative process in creating a fulfilling life with meaning and good health.

Know yourself

Creating anything is actually a risky business. This path will confront you with many challenges you didn't even know existed. It is looking into the mirror of your highest self as well as the darkest shadows. You will be confronted with your worst fears and you'll be inspired to fly to your highest heights. Creating is inviting the unknown into your life. It means being willing to go it alone because nobody else understands.

We have already explored who you are in what inspires you. This is one of our most powerful drivers to create. Knowing that we can give up too soon, let us take the time to reflect and explore in more detail what your greatest inner obstacles are. While inspiration is one of the super energies that moves us forward and will help when things get stuck, knowing our obstacles is equally vital in the creative process. Both go hand in hand.

- *What is your greatest fear?*
- *Are you afraid of what others might say or think?*
- *How they will judge you?*
- *Are you afraid of falling short of your own expectations?*
- *And what is your greatest daemon? That will make you stop just before you're there? Greed? Fear? Envy? Procrastination?*

It is worth knowing this when you engage on the creative path for a self-determined life.

Most people would probably contend that they know themselves. They define themselves through their background, upbringing, education, experience, and the environment they live in. They tend to see themselves as a fixed product with certain skills that is capable of certain things, but incapable of others.

For a highly creative person, and actually for all of us on this road of re-discovering our genius, getting to know who we are is a challenge in itself, at least when looking through the lens of our society and its current beliefs. As we can change perspective, change professions and change what we like doing, we seem to be a product in the making, a work in progress. When people ask me who I am, I have a hard time telling them. It is a constant challenge and will depend on the context and the people I'm with. There are few, if any, who I can tell about all of my achievements, all of my skills and all my careers. My father used to say "Jack of all trades and master of none." This stuck with me for most of my life and made me feel I was wrong to have so many talents, so many successful careers. I now know I was made this way and that there is a form of benevolent intelligence behind me. I can accept most of what comes with this huge package. I'm not saying everything, it's an ongoing process of uncovering more of who I am, and then learning to love that new aspect of myself as well.

It is said that it takes 20 000 hours to be a master of any trade or skill. Well, I've mastered performing, composing, painting in different styles, career coaching, to name but some activities. I'm also an expert in meditating and writing. Most of my life I've been afraid of telling people about all these skills and endeavours, because they won't take me seriously. Writing this book and understanding that this is in fact not only who I am, but potentially who we all are, has helped enormously.

Overcoming limiting beliefs and projecting another image of ourselves are prerequisites to evolving as the creative geniuses we are designed to be by nature. Our beliefs and ideas about ourselves are often rather limited, we don't see everything we are capable of. This is greatly due to our environment and upbringing. Many of us have been conditioned to lose their creative genius, and thus don't think of ourselves as highly creative, let alone understand and appreciate this gift. We think it's not possible. Our education and collective beliefs have made us into a kind of human machine. Now, with AI and digitalisation progressing, it is time to rethink who we are as human beings.

It is important to understand that living fully means changing perspective on who we are, stepping outside of our comfort zone and being daring. And by doing this, we can be the pioneers of a new age where humans begin to live their creative potential of geniuses.

It is often in a situation of crisis that we are driven to explore and develop more of our hidden potential. And, more often than not, it is life that brings opportunities we could never have dreamed of. It is also life that destroys our concepts of who we are, that shows us limitations and re-directs us to more of who we are meant to be by design. That is why, in the understanding of how we create our lives, it is important to include life as our most important partner of creation.

Every one of us is a unique instrument through which the universe creates. You can think of the universe being universal intelligence, god, chi or simply life itself. In any case, something that is greater than us. This greater force needs every one of us to create here on Earth. Because only you can bring what you are into the world. No-one else can.

To use the full range of the instrument I am and create what matters in my life, I need to fine-tune this instrument and learn to "play" it. Only I can do that. Only I know who I am, what I need, what supports me and what I would like to create. I am the expert on me. We lose a lot of energy trying to be someone else. So why not relax and blossom according to our own inherent plan.

Knowing yourself allows you to create a life that corresponds to who you truly are, not what people expect of you, nor what you think you should be doing - for whatever reasons. Knowing yourself means you can look out for yourself, your own goals, needs, ways of doing things and personal values. You will thus tap into your own wisdom and inner knowledge of what is right for you, and you only.

Knowing ourselves, in the case of a highly creative person, has to include this special talent with all its ramifications and personal consequences. And for those in the process of unleashing their creative genius energy, it needs to become a focal point. This energy and gift we all have, is so overriding and has such an incredibly huge impact that, if denied, it can destroy us, mentally or physically, or both. It needs to be acknowledged and appreciated so we can handle it.

When we talk about knowing ourselves, we need to look at that essential part of us that goes way back to when we come into this world. Rather like a seed, or blueprint in technical terms, before it has become a plant or a tree. The seed is not negotiable. It is our very essence. Our creative genius is at the core of our essence, as is our individual purpose.

We all have a purpose just like any being, animal or plant on this planet. We don't have to know it consciously, but it helps if we have a feeling for it. Our purpose over the course of a lifetime does not change. What does change is our expression of it, the way we bring it into the world. Knowing we are highly creative, we understand this can take on many forms, enabling us to explore various creative forms and expressions, and touch the lives of many different kinds of people.

Being highly creative is not negotiable. It is who we are at our deepest core. All of us.

If we want to channel our creative force in such a way that it creates meaning and wellbeing for us, it will further need to be connected to our purpose or mission in life. While everyone has a purpose, I believe, not every person has a mission. A mission is something that involves many people, that goes beyond our own personal life. Having a family can be a purpose, writing to inspire many people and change their world could be a mission.

The seed of a fig tree will always grow into a fig tree and never become an oak tree. No matter how much you treat it like an apple tree or allow others to treat it as an oak tree. It will always remain a fig tree. It will bear fruit, if nourished according to its specific needs, or die. So, if you're a fig tree, why not find out what this fig tree needs to thrive, what the conditions are that make for a lot of yummy fruit?

Giving yourself and asking others to help you create the right environment for who you truly are, will help you grow and harvest wonderful fruit, and these, in turn, will also feed others. By your very nature, you, the tree, will give your figs, year after year, to the world around you. Others can savour them, appreciate them, and use them. That is what the fig tree has to offer.

To stay with this image, knowing you are highly creative would be like the soil you need to grow in. And also knowing about what other elements you need to thrive. You will still need to embark on your individual journey to find what your specific talents and needs, likes and dislikes are, and what your purpose is. You may be a highly creative inventor, business person or a healer, and not a musician and artist like me. This process of getting to know who we are, is never-ending, and will only stop when we leave this Earth. It is an individual process as unique as you are. And it will take you to unknown territory by its very nature.

We need to find our own reason for being here, what makes us unique. No one, really no one else in the entire universe, knows what is right or good for me. I need to access my own potential, make my own choices and decisions and find my personal form of expressing, of creating, including my own way of connecting with spirit or universal intelligence for inspiration.

Many of us feel inspired by people who have "found themselves." We can sense when someone has gone into the deepest depths of their soul and has come back with new treasures. As much as the journey is individual, and there is no recipe that is valid for everyone, there is something universal about a person being authentic, and we can feel it.

Our journey may begin through imitation of such a person, until we reach that point where we realise that our path is different. We outgrow our teachers. A good teacher, like a parent, will hold a sacred space for us to experience who we are and to grow, until we can go off on our own. Our teachers and elders have travelled and know what it feels like, will recognise when we touch our core, and can support us in not giving up, not allowing doubt to stop us.

This is what I've hoped to create in this book for you. I'm one of your elders, I've created many works and career paths, I've explored creativity in its essence, and the different states of consciousness that come with it, that give us access to our creative genius. I'm no better, no worse than any other person, and I only truly know myself, I do not know who you are. I do know about the aspect of being highly creative and have learned to deal with it in my own life. And, I may add, I'm still learning every day.

Whatever we want to create needs to be meaningful to us. Meaning and purpose go together. Whereas many people seek to live their passions, finding meaning is even more powerful. It takes us beyond ourselves and connects us with the world around us, giving our lives a sense.

Expressing meaning and purpose combines my skills with what is needed in the world around me, in the unique way that is me. Bringing something that is needed into the world, for others to share, gives us profound satisfaction and a sense of purpose, perhaps even a mission.

- *What is it that you and only you can bring into the world?*
- *What is your particular song and how does it sound?*
- *What is it that you'd like to contribute to this world at the present time?*
- *Do you have a sense of your purpose? Or your mission?*

Love who you are

Loving who I am could be the most important decision I will ever take. The world needs me to appreciate who I am as I contribute my unique voice to the collective choir, creating what only I can express and which is important to me.

Loving ourselves helps us create the conditions we need to bring our essence into the world. It is also what brings life to our inborn talents, it is the motivation and the current that flows through our wiring, bringing the channel of creation to life.

We have seen how being highly creative can be perceived as not being good enough, not OK, according to the standards and demands put on us from early childhood in a society that expects and wants something else that is plannable, predictable, controllable. We have been expected to function rather like a mechanical system: if I do x it will always produce the result y. These demands are based on a mechanistic view of the world, as we have seen earlier. Together with an entirely new view of the world we live in and of us human beings, comes a new approach. One that takes into consideration our inherent genius. And, thankfully, we are beginning to see that we are not machines. We can do x and it can have a myriad of consequences, results and avenues which are by no means all plannable or predictable.

What if there is an inherent perfection in who we are, much like a tree is perfect because, and not despite, of the fact that it grows crooked or in a weird fashion? It is worth noting that we do not expect two trees of the same species to grow in exactly the same manner with branches and fruit in the same place. Every single tree is absolutely unique.

And what if the environment we are born into, with its specific set of demands and conditions, helps us develop at least part of our innate high creativity potential according to some greater plan? What if this is not random and we don't just happen to grow into who we are? And what if the conditions we are born into help us blossom into the flower we are meant to be? This does not mean, as many would probably believe, that we are encouraged, fostered and nurtured in a way that's best for us. While this may sometimes be the case, the opposite is equally true. One of my best friends had a hell of an upbringing which has turned her into a highly creative individual.

Let me share part of my upbringing and journey as an example of what I mean. I grew up in a family that moved every 1 ½ to 3 years until I was 14 years old. I went to first grade primary school three times in three different languages. I became proficient, mother tongue level, in all three. And I still managed to graduate from high school younger than everyone else in my class. From early on in my life, this lifestyle taught me to change perspective and adapt to entirely different environments. Was that the universe shaping me into a highly creative individual?

When my parents died, I was 33 and living in Switzerland, just having returned from the US. I definitely felt I had no roots. There and then I decided to grow my roots where I was. I tried to become totally Swiss, and totally like everyone around me, in an effort to find a home. It didn't work. I never felt like everyone else around me.

When I stopped performing as a musician, because it was no longer fulfilling, I began teaching languages to earn a living and I came into contact with foreigners living here. Only much later did I realise that with these people and in this environment I felt at home in many ways I hadn't before. Life had given me what I needed in a place I wasn't looking for it. I did not enjoy the teaching as such – not creative enough for me, but it provided something very precious for me: a sense of homecoming and a solid financial base to start composing, one of the most deeply satisfying and essential experiences of my life.

Let me also share some more insights into what loving ourselves may mean. As a classical musician I spent most of the first 40 years of my life striving for perfection. Practicing every single day, with very few breaks or holidays. Striving always to become more perfect technically, I realised at one point that I performed much better if I worked with the premise that I was perfect the way I was. I discovered the perfection of the soul. When my soul was expressing, technical questions moved into the background and a fresh and natural kind of perfection came forth, just like the tree growing according to its inherent nature.

I realised that there is a kind of natural beauty in each one of us. We have not learned to see it, or hear it, because our eyes and ears are trained to perceive what fits in according to certain ways and standards. We are taught to see what is missing, to look at ourselves through the eyes of others, of society and its demands. This outside perception has become so engrained into us that we have a hard time stepping out of this way of looking at ourselves and looking at ourselves from the inside.

A blossoming flower is perfect the way it is. If we imitate it on a computer in a perfect pattern, the image leaves us cold, it does not reach our soul. As I experimented with the effect images have on us, I found imperfect images that have a "natural touch" to be far more powerful than anything perfect generated by a machine. The same is true for music and its inner pulse. Remember that a healthy heart beats slightly irregularly?

Nature is not straight and perfect. As part of nature, we human beings also have a kind of perfect imperfection. We do not need to become better than our neighbour, nor more important, nor different to our inherent nature. Because of each person's uniqueness, no one can diminish the person next to them. I cannot be her and he cannot be me.

It was not until I started trying to love myself, this time consciously, that I realised how difficult it actually was. This, in spite of the fact, that by other people's standards I was doing what I loved doing: composing and painting. I realised that, deep down, I felt unloved and unappreciated. Mostly because many people, including my own family, didn't value what I was about, what I was expressing in my life, my art and my music. I could see my own beauty in what I created, but put myself down because I couldn't make others see it. I thought it was my shortcoming and my fault because I wasn't good enough.

As I got sick a good 10 years ago, and discovered the wisdom of loving myself unconditionally, I now had the huge task of changing the lens through which I had been looking at myself and my life. The new lens would be love. Another thing I realised was that if I don't love myself and appreciate myself, how can others do so? Or if they do, will I even be able to notice it, and feel it?

Loving who you are is a matter of choice. And you might as well start now, because you're not going to change who you are, in essence, no matter how much you may try. The day on which you are perfect enough to love yourself, will never come.

This is, I believe, where many self-help books fail. They make us believe that we constantly need to evolve, improve and better ourselves, and only then will we be loveable. While striving for better and more has its place, I would rather look at it this way:

Let us uncover our own perfection and beauty and bring it into the world. Let us blossom like the flower we're meant to be. A flower does not strive, does not want to improve herself. She puts everything into growing who she is meant to be. Looking at a flower fills us with awe and inspiration and joy.

The decision to love who you are will empower you to use all of your potential, including that part which you have kept hidden, those parts of you that you thought were unacceptable or out of reach, or that you condemned, for whatever reason.

This in turn will make you more perfect in the most natural way.

Loving who we are is creating space. It takes away the pressure, allowing us to naturally connect with the highest version of ourselves. Pressure and fear are the forces that separate and divide. They have their place in our lives on Earth and the duality here. However, we can always choose to change perspective, we can choose love over fear. Love connects us to something greater: to who we are, to others and to a form of universal energy.

Connected, we are so much more than alone.

I've been practising loving myself on a daily basis for many years now. It's an ongoing process, and just as life never stands still, there are always new challenges to loving myself. Paradoxically, loving what is, creates the space for change. Rather like on a hike, checking and acknowledging in a neutral way your coordinates, where you are at that moment, allows you to proceed and reach your destination from there. If I don't know where I am, I cannot find the way to where I want to go!

Whatever you come into this life with, the seed you are at birth will want to blossom at some point in this lifetime. If there remains some hidden part that has not yet grown into what it is meant to be, this part will knock on the door of your mind, heart or body. You may notice it because you see something, and it makes you feel warm and inspired. Or you hear about someone or something, and you feel attracted to it, you're keen to find out more. The same can be true for activities, places, topics etc.

Unfortunately, most of us have not learned to listen to this gentle nudge of our inner voice. We have become adept at pushing it away, ignoring it, shoving it back to where it came from. Then, life takes a turn for the unexpected: we lose our job, we get sick, someone leaves us. This is actually life cooperating with us, on its deepest level, giving us the chance to take another, deeper look inside ourselves. It makes way for us to step out of our daily routine, reflect and explore who we are. In this space we will be able to hear the inner pulse of our life. We are then more likely to open the door and welcome what we find.

Loving who we are is perhaps the greatest key to access our full potential. It is the fuel that will keep us going when faced with obstacles, fear or criticism.

Loving who we are could be the single most revolutionary act to change our world: practising it on a daily basis the most challenging, and not giving up when faced with rejection or doubt, the most sustainable.

Create what matters

If knowing ourselves is finding out how we are wired, and loving ourselves is switching on the current, then creating what matters is using that current to turn on a light, to warm up a house or mow the lawn. Creativity is an elementary force and is harnessed by knowing who we are and what matters to us. Creating based on this, will channel this power in such a way that we are fulfilled, leading a life of purpose and in good health.

In itself creativity is not positive or negative. It is pure energy and up to us to channel it. Knowing myself and loving who I am, is the focus, the channel to where I can direct this powerful energy. For a greater good as well as for my own. When we are connected deeply in this way to our essence, we can begin to create what matters.

At the same time, the more we are connected with our inherent genius of creation, the more choices and options open up, and it can become harder and more confusing to know which path to pursue.

Which option shall I chose?
Which road shall I take?

Is there a right and wrong?

Choosing and moving forward is like stepping into a torrent that could potentially be dangerous, because it's not easily manageable. This is where cooperating with life at that particular moment will act as the most practical guiding principle, once we know who we are. Inspiration and purpose are the more emotional and spiritual guiding principles that can help us focus on what matters.

Start where you are, with what's available, with existing resources. Otherwise, you risk procrastinating. In this case the energy will build up like behind a dam and potentially create havoc. It's better to do a little than nothing at all. Doing whatever is possible at that particular moment will allow you to stay in the creative flow, letting it take its course. It can then take you to where you're meant to go.

Creating what matters is a process much like parenting: after birthing and raising your creation into a „grown-up", it's time to let it go out into the world and find its place. Like children, there will be some who still need your full attention and financial support, while others are ready to earn their own money or do voluntary work.

Creating what matters, just like knowing who you are, never stops and can take you into new dimensions and untrodden paths at any moment in your life.

The perfect moment to begin

Many people never start to create because they feel some vital condition is missing in their lives. They may think: "When I have enough money, I will set up a business" or "When I've tidied up my small flat and have a designated area, I will start to paint". This perfect moment in time, when all conditions are perfect, will never come. If you have this kind of internal dialogue, just turn it around: "I will set up my own business and then earn money" and "I will start painting on the corner of a table and then I'll tidy up." Because beginning to create really motivates us: having felt the pleasure of painting, I'm motivated to create more space for it. Having set up my business and either stopped working in my regular job or working less, I'm really pushed to make money in this new way.

What is something you've been wanting to do and where you've waited for the perfect conditions before starting?

As a teenager I had piano and flute lessons. The flute my parents bought for me was pretty much the cheapest there was, but absolutely fine. After all we were four children. When many years later I wanted to study music to become a professional musician, I only had this instrument and no money to buy an appropriate instrument, which would have cost me at least 6'000 to 8'000 CHF in those days - now it's a lot more. This didn't stop me. And because I was OK with it, no-one else seemed to mind much. The universe stepped in with a most unlikely unplannable scheme. I married a man who was widowed. He had kept his ex-wife's belongings and amongst them was a high-quality flute worth 10'000 CHF. He lent it to me for the duration of our time together which lasted until I graduated with my flute diploma. Then, after our divorce and him taking back the flute, a student stepped in and lent me the money to buy one for myself. I paid this off in very small affordable amounts, as I was not earning a lot as a young professional freelance musician. There are more turns and twists to this story, but ultimately, I landed a prestigious scholarship to do my Master's in Music at Boston University. To earn a bit of cash before going there, I worked as an interpreter for an American businessman at a trade fair. We got together as a couple and he paid off the remaining amount due for my flute.

Why am I telling you this? I strongly believe that intention paves the way for creation. If I seriously intend to do something and do everything I possibly can to create the desired result, even if it doesn't happen then, at some point, and often in mysterious ways, it will happen. In some cases, for me it has been decades later.

Once you know what it is you want to bring into this world, this intention is like a seed. Doing anything and everything you possibly can at the present moment to make it come alive within the conditions you are in at that particular time, equals putting it in the right soil and watering it. In my experience, there then often comes a break. This is when germination begins, when we need to let go, and allow the universe to step in. This may happen fairly quickly, like within days, or it may take decades. I have experienced all of these time frames.

Life, when we least expect it, offers us opportunities. Often not in the form we would have envisaged them, sometimes not even obvious as something we would want. Luckily, we have our different brains that we have learned to trust by now. There is a gut feeling about opportunities that life presents us with. We just know this is the right moment and the right offer to take on. It is not always an easy decision, contrary to what we may think. It can feel challenging, almost impossible. The head may well find good reasons to opt out.

Often, the amount of fear equals the energy of the desire. If it is something we've longed for and worked towards, and is deeply connected to who we are, it can be really scary. There is just so much at stake. What if after all this time it doesn't give me pleasure, or I'm no good at it?

Usually, the inner urge and the anticipated joy are stronger than the associated fear. Something inside of us knows when it's right for us.

When I was asked to coach executives and specialists who had lost their jobs, it was not anything I consciously wanted or had worked towards. Had I not been ill, stopped all of my professional activities and been in need of money, I may not have said yes. And yet, it was exactly what one part of me wanted. A good ten years prior to this, when teaching languages to business people, I had declared wanting to bring my tools and processes developed over the course of my creative life, into the business world. And here was my chance to do so – not at all the way I had envisioned it I may add. I've had to make it my own by using my mental and visualisation techniques, as well as all the other approaches I had developed. People love it.

New creative ventures often come in disguise and profoundly challenge us. They rarely come the way we envisioned them. As a highly creative person, we need to embark periodically on these new quests and ventures.

Here is a great paradox, and something for those of you who are highly creative, to remember. Persons who are "simply" creative have an easier time expressing their creativity. There is much less pressure, there is no hidden iceberg underneath. Highly Creative Persons, however, instinctively feel that being creative is who they are, it's like exposing yourself naked to the world.

So, start small with no expectations, enjoy the process, the flow, and don't focus on the result! Once you've experienced the thrill of being in a creative flow, that will act as your motivation, rather than "producing" a specific result. Remember, producing a desired result is the old way of functioning, the mechanical one.

This is a fine line, once again, between having an idea of what you wish to create and allowing the creative life force to step in and take you there. Both aspects are indeed necessary for a satisfactory result: me and the creative energy. In the more spiritual scene, some people channel energies without filter, without using their own sense of what is right or wrong. It is important to be a conscious channel, one with integrity and a sense of ethics, of what is right for you and what isn't. This will channel the creative energy in keeping with who you are. If in doubt, let love be your highest compass.

It is now time to think about how to express your unique quality in the world and take the first step in creating what matters to you.

When the next step, the way forward, eludes us, it's good to create the space and time to listen to what your different brains have to say on the matter.

- *Is there an impulse, like writing down something, going somewhere, or talking to someone?*
- *Is there something you'd love to do, a movie you'd like to see? A place you'd like to visit?*
- *Do you want to call an old friend? Pick up a pencil and start drawing?*

The impulse can seem totally unconnected to your question of what you want to create. Follow it anyway. All of this is part of the way forward. It is one stepping stone that can lead to undreamed-of next steps.

The whole path in front of us needn't be clear in order for us to begin. Just take that one step. Act on that one impulse and follow your heart!

Entering the creative zone: our sacred space

When you step into the unknown, you allow the cycle of creation to begin. Letting go and entering the void can be the first step in creating your next work of art, project or meaningful pursuit.

As highly creative individuals, our heads are often full of ideas, we're raring to go and sometimes overcharged with our creative power. Everything we do tends to trigger our creativity and the desire to do things our own way, whether it's cleaning, doing admin or meeting friends. This means it's a challenge to fully relax, to do activities that don't demand anything but presence, to play.

But being creative is as much about expressing as it is about receiving, opening up and being passive. It is about being totally present in the moment and allowing that energy to move us to express through the unique channel that we are.

For our own balance and sanity, it is vital we find spaces, activities, rituals and routines to re-source ourselves and to express who we truly are in an easily flowing manner. This is not always found in our profession, business or the actual creative project we're working on. We need a kind of sanctuary where no one and nothing matters but our very own selves, our core and essence. This is where our creative juices and ideas come from, as we enter our most creative zone, where we're not putting any pressure or expectations on ourselves.

These sanctuaries can be places where we feel good, activities that allow us to express without thinking, and things we love doing.

For our creative juices to flow, we also need to regularly empty our brains and refill them with inspiration. Any form of meditation facilitates access to these other dimensions. It allows us to suspend what we call reason and access the creative energy directly.

In our modern Western world, we are generally more concerned with transmitting and being active than receiving and being passive. It seems more gratifying. Pursuing our goals, we are asked to be active and tend to forget that receiving is just as important. The same approach pervades all of our society and endeavours, including the arts and music.

Laotse calls this emptiness-fullness the Tao, modern science calls it The Field. It is the gateway through which things manifest, including miracles. The Tao is the womb, the mystery. The Field theory tells us we are connected to everything that is. There is no separation between them and us. So, it seems quite logical that there is a correspondence between the outer and our inner world. Communicating with the Field, or if you prefer the divine, conveys a sense of being joined together invisibly and of being part of something greater.

It may be a good idea to actually physically create a space where you can meditate, find inspiration and connect to that which inspires you, in whatever form is right for you. A place that is always there when you need it. Your sanctuary just for yourself, to reflect, create, or simply do nothing. A playroom, your breathing space. If you don't have space in your home, this can be in nature. Go to your favourite tree, sit by the water undisturbed and meditate, watch the river flow, gurgle and bubble, as it flows...

When we look into water or at clouds, watching their movements and changing forms, our analytical minds are busy observing, allowing another part of us to open up the border between our conscious and the subconscious mind. We can enter into the huge reservoir of information not accessible in our normal active "doing" modus. We access this zone in meditation, in music, in flow and artistic creation, through images, and when we go for walks in nature.

I call these creative spaces 'sacred'. Why sacred? There is something profoundly holy about entering these spaces. This is the core of creation, where alchemistic processes take place, where straw turns into gold metaphorically speaking. We find 'gold' in the form of insight or inspiration and, by connecting to a higher form of intelligence and love, we encounter spirit. A profoundly mystical and personal experience.

We used to go to church or to a temple to experience this connection. And some of us still do. But we can be in awe of creation anywhere. As much in nature, listening to music, in the act of creating, or in front of a work of art.

DOING IT MY WAY

ooking back, I not only see how I tried to fit into a specific culture to belong here in Switzerland, but I finally recognise that I was always trying to do things the way "they were supposed to be done". It has taken me more than 60 years to understand that this could equally be connected to my highly creative wiring and energy, and not just my upbringing in many different cultures, with different languages.

When I auditioned with the Principal Flutist of the Boston Symphony Orchestra to study with her on my Fulbright scholarship, she listened to my playing and the first comment she made was: "I'm going to teach you to play within the limits of the flute". That actually says it all!

Unfortunately, there was no shortcut for me, as there isn't for anyone. All of the multifaceted, joyful and painful experiences of my life have brought me to where I am now. I can finally love myself for who I am. And the process will never stop. That is what being highly creative is about.

Doing things my own way applies to all aspects of my life. In my professional life this has not only meant being successful in several careers, it has also meant that I've been self-employed almost my entire life. I've never been able to work long hours in any structure, such as an orchestra, music school etc., always needing a lot of free time around any such commitment. However, when absorbed by my own project, inspired to the maximum and in the flow of creating, I can focus intensely over long periods of time.

As a young married woman, and later musician, I sewed my own clothes – not realising at the time that this was my creative expression. I often went on till early morning, not able to stop before the garment was finished. Even if it meant undoing a mistake and redoing it. It was like being in a tunnel – quite obsessive.

Doing it my way has also meant healing from minor and major illnesses my own way.

In my early 50s I had excruciating pains in my right shoulder, the after-effects of dislocating my shoulder several times as a teenager, several operations, and decades of playing the flute, sculpting and painting. The specialist I consulted told me there was only one solution: a new joint. But even then, he couldn't guarantee the pain would be gone.

Here I was, feeling like my life was over. If I couldn't compose, play the piano, paint and write, what was left in my life?

I felt old and depressed…. Until I decided this was the time to apply all the things I had learned over the course of a lifetime: my mental and relaxation techniques, music and visualising. I created a CD with my own music and recorded my voice telling me how I was able to play the piano, play volleyball and more.

A year later the mother of a student invited me to play basketball. It was a very lonely period in my life. Lonely and lost – I wouldn't ever want to go back there. I told her I couldn't because of my shoulder. She said I could play any way I wanted to, they were easy going, not ambitious and strict. I went, played my own way and even managed to score throwing baskets from below rather than above, and generally had a good time. I left exhilarated: I had actually achieved my goal of being able to play, not volleyball but basketball. That was definitely good enough for me!

Since then, I've been able to paint, compose and write. I even started swimming last year. Painful though it is, I do it because it makes me feel good.

Here's an important aspect of healing and perhaps of all creative ventures: the result does not have to be perfect. If it's good enough, that's fine. If I'm able to transmit my essence, perfect for me!

Creative healing

A special and vital aspect of human creativity is our ability to heal in a creative way. The mechanistic view of the world and ourselves has led us to believe that our bodies are machines, that parts need to be fixed for the whole to function and, if necessary, be replaced completely. The medicine we take is the same for everyone, including the dose. The assumption is that as machines we all function in the exact same way.

What if things are actually not like this? What if healing, becoming whole, is an individual process that is highly creative? What if our bodies are intelligent by design and what we term "illness" is the body's inherent way of becoming healthy, the symptoms being part of the healing process? Our bodies are highly creative in ways we haven't even begun to understand. In a world where everything is connected can we see how we can not only communicate with our bodies, but also understand that we are first and foremost souls and spirits in a body? If the soul is traumatised, hurt or otherwise out of balance, our bodies respond and enable us to enter into a dialogue of healing.

Modern medicine is slowly and tentatively beginning to explore what has been termed miracle healings. They are beginning to see that actually in these miracles nature and universal intelligence are at work, that this is the way we are meant to function. That there are aspects vital for healing and living that have been taken out of the equation in modern medicine.

Understanding this means that each one of us, and every "illness", is here for a reason, pointing out what needs to be healed not only in my body, but also in my mind and in my emotions.

This implies that there is an act of creativity involved in healing. We don't all deal with traumas, hardships and other injuries or mishaps life brings us in the same way. What is true for other aspects of life, obviously also applies here: how we perceive the "illness", how we approach the healing process, the action we take or don't take. All of this affects how we get well or don't.

In my life, I have healed in many different ways. I've used traditional Western medicine as well as alternative routes, energy healing, body therapies, mental techniques and much more. I am not advocating a specific approach here. The only thing I do know is that my body can heal itself and it is my job to support it in this process. What works for me, doesn't necessarily work for you.

I have shared the story of healing my shoulder. Perhaps I can inspire you to explore your very personal journey of healing by sharing some more stories. One major illness was about ten years ago, when I was really terrified of dying. I did use traditional medicine for a minor operation. However, when they suggested I do a major invasive operation that would have affected me for the rest of my life, plus severe medication for two years that would have had such side effects as to make life miserable, I opted out.

Instead, I listened to my own inner wisdom telling me it was time to love myself unconditionally, like I had learned to love others. This has been the major "remedy" which, to this day, has kept me healthy. I am extremely grateful that I was able to listen to this inner voice despite my fear. Perhaps leading a life where intuition has played a central role helped in such an extreme situation.

So do start now with all the tools and process you wish to develop. Like with any skill, it's easier to learn when you're not under pressure.

A few years ago, I went to see a new dentist, a more holistic one. He told me I had a black spot inside my mouth that needed regular checks. After my illness ten years ago, I was once again terrified. Having practiced visualising and feeling completely healthy over the years since that first operation, I saw the inside of my mouth in a healthy red colour. A few months later, when I went to see him again to check on this spot, it was gone! I also had a black spot on my lip which wasn't so much scary as simply ugly, making me feel old and undesirable. This, too, disappeared, over the course of several months.

I believe that creative healing is our future. We will understand this immense potential we possess to heal with the innate healing ability and intelligence our bodies possess.

TO THE MOON AND BEYOND: THE LIFE OF A HIGHLY CREATIVE PERSON

Typically for a highly creative person, there are many different threads woven into the fabric of one's life. I have already shared some of them on this journey together. Let me share here some more threads of my life to illustrate the complexity of the co-creating process in our life as Highly Creative Persons – and potentially for anyone setting out to uncover our inherent genius. It is my story of how life took me by the hand, and together we went to the moon and beyond. I achieved more than I ever would have imagined possible.

Music, when I was 15, was an inner home for me. When playing and practicing classical music on the piano and the flute, I slipped into my own world. One moment stands out to this day and has proved to be a kind of undercurrent of my life. I was thinking: "How do you create this kind of music?" It seemed the greatest mystery, rather like imagining myself flying to the moon. It wasn't that I dreamed of becoming a composer, there was just this question wanting to be explored. Was this a first hint at my creative potential, unbeknown to myself?

While my life unfolded, I forgot about it entirely. I studied languages first, and only later music, and finally became a professional musician with a successful career, performing and teaching internationally. After a while, something unexpressed prompted me to start painting and sculpting. Thus began my second career as an artist, before giving up performing altogether. I had achieved all I wanted as a performer on the flute.

Then, after exploring my creativity and artistic expression through visual art, I felt ready to start creating my own music. I envisioned myself recording what I was playing and using that, rather than the traditional method of writing down music. This is indeed possible now, but not in those days. It would take another 10 years.

Unable to do it my way, I forgot about music... Until 2001 a former colleague asked me whether I would take over her piano class, as she wanted to go on a sabbatical. I had not been active as a classical musician for years, and she was asking me to take on a piano class, although I was a flutist. This was quite mysterious. The job proved to be a real gift from heaven: it offered me the chance to participate in an improvisation workshop for pianists, organised through the music school. It felt as if I had waited all my life for this moment. I just knew I had to go there.

After the course, I went on a search to find the right equipment to record my improvisations. As a classically trained musician, I was not familiar with e-pianos, keyboards and synthesizers, but after trying out many different instruments, I finally found the right instrument for what I had in mind. It turned out that the project was on hold again, because I didn't have the means to pay for it.

A year later, my new boyfriend asked me to come to a trade fair with him. I wasn't really keen on going but went along because it was something to do together. There, amidst skis and pots and pans, I discovered a stand selling keyboards. Out of the 4-5 models on display, one of them was the exact one I had chosen a year before. Excited, I showed it to him. And, there and then, he bought it for me!

I now had my instrument, but no clue how to operate it.

Life weaved some more magic into this story through the visit of my oldest musician friend, a highly successful classical violin player. After we had enjoyed a good meal, she surprised me by wanting to play some music together. It had been several years since I had been active as a flutist. Somehow, I mustered the courage to tell her I'd rather play the piano, though I certainly wasn't up to her professional standard on this instrument. After playing a Schubert sonata, my friend suggested I needed to pursue my piano playing. This meant a lot to me. I contacted a violinist I'd worked with, who agreed right away, and she also organised a cellist for us to form a trio. Overnight, another one of my dreams had come true. I would be playing chamber music on the piano - as a teenager I had seen myself as a pianist, rather than as a flutist. What's more, it was absolutely amazing how well I could play these difficult trios, in spite of the fact that I had not practised all those years. I now played better than ever, and it filled me with unspeakable joy.

We began to improvise, using my keyboard which, apart from helping me gain more experience improvising, also enabled me to get to know the technical aspects of this instrument. After about a year, I wanted to move on to something more professional. The violinist didn't, unfortunately. She was not a professional musician.

Lonely and very disappointed, I sat down at my keyboard, thinking: "This means, I will have to continue on my own". And that is when I started composing, with my very own process of composition/ improvisation. A few months later, I completed and published my first CD with my own music. This was in 2004.

There were more mysterious threads woven into this story that allowed me „to fly to the moon", composing my own music. But for the purpose of what I'd like to share, let me continue.

Life, and a kind of universal intelligence, had guided me, inspired me and helped my life unfold in a totally unpredictable way, full of magic and mystery, to this point. It had more in store for me.

About 10 years later, I became seriously ill. This made me doubt everything I had done in my life so far. Shouldn't I be healthy and well, having achieved what I had? Having led a creative and spiritual life? I had learned to know myself, I had followed my intuition, and I had co-created with life. What was „missing"?

The answer came from inside: I had learned to love others unconditionally, but not myself. I now learned that loving myself means loving who I've become, what my life looks like, the choices I've made that brought me here, including everything I don't have. Loving myself has become my daily practice. It has opened up a whole new life. Another creative venture began, which has resulted in me coaching business executives and highly trained specialists, helping them through crises in their careers and with health challenges. It has culminated in another creative project: I have written and published my second book.

And now, in this third book, I am finally weaving all the threads of my life together, having realised how my secret potential of being highly creative has been at the core of all my experiences. It is what has driven me to express, explore and create. Never in my wildest dreams could I have ever imagined any of this. It is beyond anything conceivable, just like the music I was playing as a teenager. This is what heaven on earth looks like for me. I am blessed and grateful that life has, through many challenges I didn't know how to master, unwanted illnesses and unforeseen help, brought me here.

Recently I embarked on another creative journey that began 15 years ago. After exploiting all the sounds my keyboard had to offer, I had to find a new way of composing. I sidestepped into composing songs with piano accompaniment. It was only late last year that I found the equipment that offers me all of that in a way that doesn't take away from the creative process. I'm not a person interested in technical feasibility, I just want to use tech in a practical way. Finally, I have taken up the music I started composing 15 years ago and am recording it with my voice. This is really scary and I'm grateful that

I have tools and processes, insights into the creative and expressive process that help me through this.

Life is making me use a whole new part of my potential that I didn't know I had. Over and over again. It has taken me to the moon… and beyond! And, what's more, I know it will keep doing so until the moment I leave this wonderful world.

If you'd like to explore this topic more, connect with Tessa and discover her resources, please visit:

www.oursecretpotential.com
or
www.highly-creative.com